# SINGING OUR FAITH

## A Hymnal for Young Catholics

GIA PUBLICATIONS, INC.
CHICAGO

# PREFACE

The purpose of this collection of hymns, psalms and songs is two-fold and quite uncomplicated. It is a collection of musical and liturgical resources designed to enable today's children to pray and worship in song, and it is a collection of musical and liturgical resources which they will carry with them into Christian adulthood. With that double purpose in mind, the editors have carefully chosen materials which both appeal to children and have a timelessness which they will not outgrow. This is both a repertoire for use in schools and catechetical settings, and a collection of material that is at the core of a healthy adult parish repertoire.

Special recognition for this project goes to Jeffry Mickus, production coordinator; Philip Roberts, music engraver; Victoria Krstansky and Clarence Reiels, proofreaders; Laura Cacciottolo, copyright permissions; and Robert H. Oldershaw, topical index.

Robert J. Batastini
      Senior Editor / Project Director
David Anderson
Sr. Teresita Espinosa, CSJ
Rob Glover
Robert W. Piercy, Jr.
      Editors

Cover art by Yolanda Duran.

Published with approval of the Commitee on the Liturgy, National Conference of Catholic Bishops.

ISBN 1-57999-113-0

   4 5 6 7 8 9 10 11 12 13 14 15 16 17 18 19 20

# Contents

## Daily Prayer

## Hymns and Songs

## Indexes

* These indexes only appear in the cantor/guitar and accompaniment editions.

# A Note to Children

This is your book of sacred songs. These are songs of our faith. Ours is a faith that people all around the world share and celebrate. God is our Father, Jesus Christ is Lord, and the Holy Spirit fills us with grace to share our gifts.

The people who put this book together chose songs you could sing for years to come. You will sing these sacred songs when you are young and you can share these sacred songs some day should you have children of your own.

There are many different types of songs in this book. Some are about the seasons of the church year like Advent, Christmas, Lent, and Easter. Some will tell stories about creation, God, Jesus, and the sacraments. We will sing about how we as the church must help all the people of the world. There is also a special section where you will find songs about our blessed Mother Mary, the saints, angels, and even a section of songs you can sing as blessings.

At the beginning of this hymnal you will find songs and prayers for the beginning and the end of the day. A special section contains psalms, which are songs with words taken from one book in the Bible. Psalms are meant to be sung, and you will find fifty psalms in this hymnal. The next section contains music which we sing in each and every Mass, such as the Holy, Holy. The rest of the songs, some of which we call hymns, follow.

Take some time to look at the cover of this book. The artist, Yolanda Duran, made it especially for you. Notice the many colors and all the things that are happening. How many children can you find? What are some of the children doing? Do you do these things in church? Take time to see if these things look like anything that happens when you pray together. Do you notice how everyone is singing or playing an instrument?

All of us at GIA Publications, Inc. are happy to know you are SINGING OUR FAITH. If you would ever like to write to us and let us know what you think, please contact us at:

Singing Our Faith
GIA Publications, Inc.
7404 S. Mason Ave.
Chicago, IL 60638

Enjoy and Sing Out Gladly!

# Daily Prayer

## PRAYER TO BEGIN THE DAY

*We make the sign of the cross as the leader begins:*
Lord, open my lips.

*Assembly:*
**And my mouth will proclaim your praise.**

*All:*
**Glory to the Father, and to the Son, and to the Holy Spirit:**
**as it was in the beginning, is now and will be for ever. Amen.**
*(Outside Lent:* **Alleluia.***)*

## MORNING HYMN 2

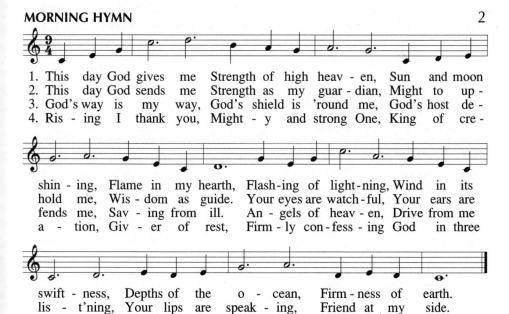

1. This day God gives me Strength of high heav - en, Sun and moon shin - ing, Flame in my hearth, Flash-ing of light-ning, Wind in its swift - ness, Depths of the o - cean, Firm-ness of earth.
2. This day God sends me Strength as my guar - dian, Might to up - hold me, Wis - dom as guide. Your eyes are watch - ful, Your ears are lis - t'ning, Your lips are speak - ing, Friend at my side.
3. God's way is my way, God's shield is 'round me, God's host de - fends me, Sav - ing from ill. An - gels of heav - en, Drive from me al - ways All that would harm me, Stand by me still.
4. Ris - ing I thank you, Might - y and strong One, King of cre - a - tion, Giv - er of rest, Firm - ly con - fess - ing God in three Per - sons, One - ness of God - head, Trin - i - ty blest.

Text: Ascribed to St. Patrick; James Quinn, SJ, b.1919, © 1969. Used by permission of Selah Publishing Co., Inc., Kingston, NY 12401, North
American agent.
Tune: BUNESSAN, 5 5 5 4 D; Gaelic; acc. by Robert J. Batastini, b.1942, © 1999, GIA Publications, Inc.

# PSALMODY

## 3   PSALM 146

Refrain

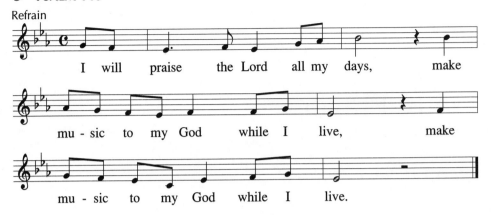

I will praise the Lord all my days, make
mu - sic to my God while I live, make
mu - sic to my God while I live.

Verses

1. Put no trust in the powerful, mere mortals in whom there is no help.
   Take their breath, they return to clay, and their plans that day come to nothing.
   They are happy who are helped by Jacob's God, whose hope is in the Lord their God,
   who alone made heaven and earth, the seas and all they contain.

2. It is the Lord who keeps faith for ever, who is just to the oppressed.
   It is God who gives bread to the hungry, the Lord, who sets prisoners free.
   It is the Lord who gives sight to the blind, who raises up those who are bowed down,
   the Lord who protects the stranger, and upholds the widow and orphan.

3. It is the Lord who loves the just but thwarts the path of the wicked.
   The Lord will reign for ever, Zion's God from age to age.

Text: Psalm 146; The Grail, © 1963, 1993, GIA Publications, Inc., agent
Tune: Michael Joncas, b.1951, © 1990, GIA Publications, Inc.

## PSALM PRAYER

# WORD OF GOD

## CANTICLE OF ZACHARY (BENEDICTUS)

1. Now ✠ bless the God of Is - ra - el, Who comes in love and pow'r, Who rais - es from the roy - al house De - liv - 'rance in this hour. Through ho - ly proph - ets God has sworn To free us from a - larm, To save us from the heav - y hand Of all who wish us harm.

2. Re - mem - ber - ing the cov - e - nant, God res - cues us from fear, That we might serve in ho - li - ness And peace from year to year; And you, my child, shall go be - fore To preach, to proph - e - sy, That all may know the ten - der love, The grace of God most high.

3. In ten - der mer - cy, God will send The day - spring from on high, Our ris - ing sun, the light of life For those who sit and sigh. God comes to guide our way to peace, That death shall reign no more. Sing prais - es to the Ho - ly One! O wor - ship and a - dore!

Text: *Benedictus,* Luke 1:68-79; Ruth Duck, b.1947, © 1992, GIA Publications, Inc.
Tune: FOREST GREEN, CMD; English; harm. by Michael Joncas, b.1951, © 1987, GIA Publications, Inc.

**INTERCESSIONS**

**OUR FATHER**

**CONCLUDING PRAYER**

**BLESSING**

## 5  PRAYER TO END THE DAY

*We make the sign of the cross as the leader begins:*
God, come to my assistance.

*Assembly:*
**Lord, make haste to help me.**

*All:*
**Glory to the Father, and to the Son, and to the Holy Spirit:**
**as it was in the beginning, is now and will be for ever. Amen.**
*(Outside Lent:* **Alleluia.***)*

## 6  EVENING HYMN

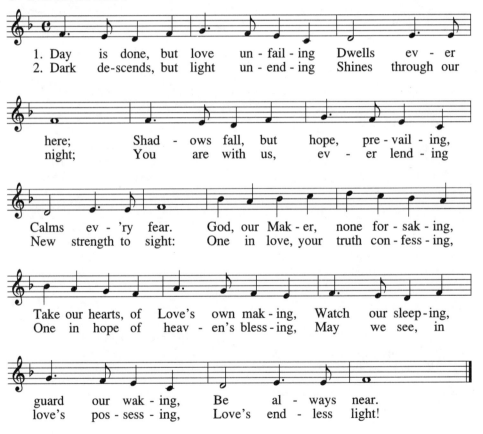

1. Day is done, but love un-fail-ing Dwells ev - er
2. Dark de-scends, but light un-end-ing Shines through our

here; Shad - ows fall, but hope, pre - vail - ing,
night; You are with us, ev - er lend - ing

Calms ev - 'ry fear. God, our Mak - er, none for - sak - ing,
New strength to sight: One in love, your truth con - fess - ing,

Take our hearts, of Love's own mak - ing, Watch our sleep-ing,
One in hope of heav - en's bless-ing, May we see, in

guard our wak - ing, Be al - ways near.
love's pos - sess - ing, Love's end - less light!

Text: James Quinn, SJ, b.1919, © 1969. Used by permission of Selah Publishing Co., Inc., Kingston, NY 12401, North American agent.
Tune: AR HYD Y NOS, 8 4 8 4 888 4; Welsh

# PSALMODY

## PSALM 121

7

Antiphon

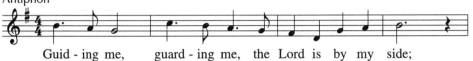

Guid - ing me,  guard - ing me,  the Lord is  by  my  side;

guid - ing me,  guard - ing me,  the Lord up - holds my  life.

Verses

1. I lift up my eyes to the mountains;
   from where shall come my help?
   My help shall come from the Lord my God
   who made heaven and earth.

2. May he never allow you to stumble!
   Let him sleep not, your guard.
   No, he sleeps not nor slumbers,
   he, Israel's guard.

3. The Lord is your guard and your shade;
   at your right side he stands.
   By day the sun shall not smite you
   nor the moon in the night.

4. The Lord will guard you from evil,
   he will guard your soul.
   The Lord will guard your going and coming
   both now and for ever.

5. Praise the Father, the Son and Holy Spirit,
   both now and for ever,
   the God who is, who was and who will be,
   world without end.

Text: Psalm 121, Michael Joncas, b.1951
Tune: Michael Joncas, b.1951
© 1988, GIA Publications, Inc.

## PSALM PRAYER

# WORD OF GOD

## 8 CANTICLE OF MARY (MAGNIFICAT)

1. My ✠ heart sings out with joy - ful praise To God who rais - es
2. The arm of God is strong and just To scat - ter all the
3. The prom - ise made in a - ges past At last has come to

me, Who came to me when I was low And
proud. The ty - rants tum - ble from their thrones And
be, For God has come in pow'r to save, To

changed my des - ti - ny. The Ho - ly One, the
van - ish like a cloud. The hun - gry all are
set all peo - ple free. Re - mem - b'ring those who

Liv - ing God, Is al - ways full of grace To those who
sat - is - fied; The rich are sent a - way. The poor of
wait to see Sal - va - tion's dawn-ing day, Our Sav - ior

seek their Mak-er's will In ev - 'ry time and place.
earth who suf - fer long Will wel - come God's new day.
comes to all who weep To wipe their tears a - way.

Text: *Magnificat,* Luke 1:46-55; Ruth Duck, b.1947, © 1992, GIA Publications, Inc.
Tune: KINGSFOLD, CMD; English traditional; harm. by Ralph Vaughan Williams, 1872-1958, © Oxford University Press

**INTERCESSIONS**

**OUR FATHER**

**CONCLUDING PRAYER**

**BLESSING**

# Psalm Refrains

Psalm 19: The Precepts of the Lord (RG)  9

The pre-cepts of the Lord give joy to the heart.

Psalm 19: Their Message Goes Out (RG)  10

Their mes-sage goes out through all the earth.

Psalm 23: The Lord Is My Shepherd (RS)  11

The Lord is my shep-herd, I shall not want. The

Lord is my shep-herd, I shall not want.

Psalm 23: My Shepherd Is the Lord (JG)  12

My shep-herd is the Lord, noth-ing in-deed shall I want.

Psalm 24: We Long to See Your Face (KK)  13

O God, this is the peo-ple that longs to see your face. O

God, this is the peo-ple that longs to see your face.

14 *Psalm 24: Open Wide Your Gates (KK)*

O-pen wide your gates; Let the King of Glo - ry in!

O-pen wide your gates; Let the King of Glo - ry in!

15 *Psalm 25: To You, O Lord (MH)*

To you, O Lord, I lift my soul, to you, I lift my soul.

16 *Psalm 25: Teach Me Your Ways (DH)*

Teach me your ways, O Lord.

17 *Psalm 27: The Lord Is My Light (DH)*

The Lord is my light and my sal - va - tion, of

whom should I be a - fraid, of whom should I be a - fraid?

18 *Psalm 27: I Long to See Your Face (RG)*

I long to see your face, O Lord.

19 *Psalm 33: Lord, Let Your Mercy (MG)*

Lord, let your mer-cy be on us, as we place our trust in you.

20 *Psalm 34: Taste and See (MG)*

Taste and see the good - ness of the Lord.

Psalm 34: The Lord Hears the Cry of the Poor (MG)   21

The Lord hears the cry of the poor.

Psalm 34: The Lord Set Me Free (RG)   22

The Lord set me free from all my fears.

Psalm 40: Here Am I (RP)   23

Here am I, Lord; I come to do your will.

Psalm 51: Be Merciful, O Lord (PC)   24

Be mer - ci-ful, O Lord, for we have sinned.

Psalm 63: My Soul Is Thirsting (RP)   25

My soul is thirst-ing for you, O

Lord, thirst-ing for you my God.

Psalm 63: In the Morning I Will Sing (DCI)   26

In the morn - ing I will sing, will

sing glad songs of praise to you.

Psalm 78: The Lord Gave Them Bread (MG)   27

The Lord gave them bread from heav - en.

28 *Psalm 78: Do Not Forget (RJB)*

Do not for - get the works of the Lord!

29 *Psalm 84: How Lovely Is Your Dwelling Place (AGM)*

How love - ly is your dwell-ing place, Lord, might-y God.

30 *Psalm 89: For Ever I Will Sing (JRC)*

For ev - er I will sing the good - ness of the Lord.

31 *Psalm 90: In Every Age (EE)*

In ev-'ry age, O Lord, you have been our ref - uge.

32 *Psalm 90: Fill Us with Your Love (RJB)*

Fill us with your love, O Lord, and we will sing for joy!

33 *Psalm 91: Be with Me (MH)*

Be with me, Lord, when I am in troub-le, be with me, Lord, I pray.

34 *Psalm 95: Let Us Come Before the Lord (RJB)*

Let us come be - fore the Lord and praise him.

35 *Psalm 96: Proclaim to All the Nations (DH)*

Pro-claim to all the na-tions the mar - vel-ous deeds of the Lord!

Pro-claim to all the na-tions the mar-vel-ous deeds of the Lord!

*Psalm 98: All the Ends of the Earth (DH, MH)* 36

All the ends of the earth have seen the pow-er of God;

all the ends of the earth have seen the pow-er of God.

*Psalm 98: Sing to the Lord a New Song (MG)* 37

Sing to the Lord a new song, for he has done mar-vel-ous deeds.

*Psalm 100: We Are God's People (DH)* 38

We are God's peo - ple, the flock of the Lord.

*Psalm 104: Lord, Send Out Your Spirit (PL)* 39

\*1.   2.   3.   4.

Lord, send out your Spir-it, and re - new the face of the earth!

*\*May be sung as a canon.*

*Psalm 113: Blessed Be the Name (RJB)* 40

Bless-ed be the name of the Lord for ev-er, and ev-er.

*Psalm 117: Go Out to All the World (AP)* 41

Go out to all the world, and tell the Good News.

42 *Psalm 118: Let Us Rejoice (MH)*

This is the day the Lord has made, let us re-joice and be glad;
*Or:* Al - le-lu-ia, al - le - lu - ia! Al - le - lu - ia!

this is the day the Lord has made, let us re-joice and be glad!
Al - le-lu - ia, al - le - lu - ia! Al - le - lu - ia!

43 *Psalm 119: Happy are They (RG)*

Hap-py are they who fol-low the law of the Lord.

44 *Psalm 121: Our Help Comes from the Lord (MJ)*

Our help comes from the Lord, the mak-er of heav-en and earth.

45 *Psalm 122: Let Us Go Rejoicing (MJ)*

Let us go re - joic-ing to the house of the Lord;

Let us go re - joic-ing to the house of the Lord.

46 *Psalm 122: Give Peace, O Lord (RG)*

Give peace, O Lord, to those who wait for you.

47 *Psalm 126: The Lord Has Done Great Things (RP)*

The Lord has done great things for us;

we are filled with joy, we are filled with joy.

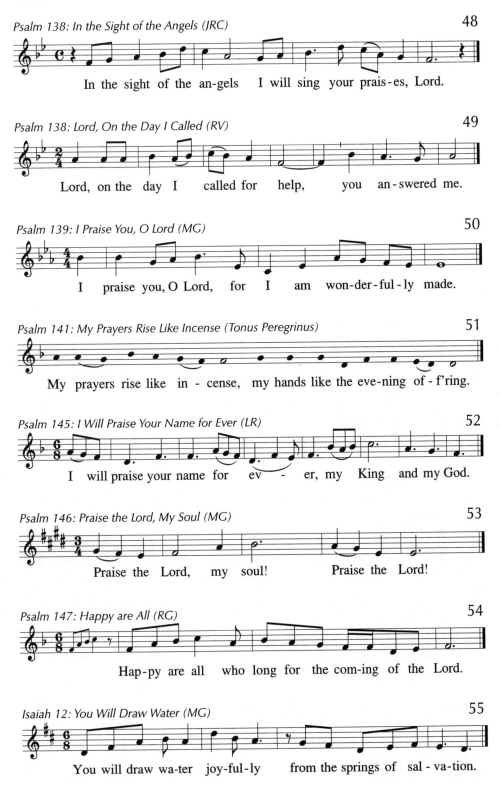

Psalm 138: In the Sight of the Angels (JRC) — 48

In the sight of the an-gels I will sing your prais-es, Lord.

Psalm 138: Lord, On the Day I Called (RV) — 49

Lord, on the day I called for help, you an-swered me.

Psalm 139: I Praise You, O Lord (MG) — 50

I praise you, O Lord, for I am won-der-ful-ly made.

Psalm 141: My Prayers Rise Like Incense (Tonus Peregrinus) — 51

My prayers rise like in-cense, my hands like the eve-ning of-f'ring.

Psalm 145: I Will Praise Your Name for Ever (LR) — 52

I will praise your name for ev - er, my King and my God.

Psalm 146: Praise the Lord, My Soul (MG) — 53

Praise the Lord, my soul! Praise the Lord!

Psalm 147: Happy are All (RG) — 54

Hap-py are all who long for the com-ing of the Lord.

Isaiah 12: You Will Draw Water (MG) — 55

You will draw wa-ter joy-ful-ly from the springs of sal-va-tion.

# Service Music

## 56 RITE OF SPRINKLING

Refrain

Springs of wa-ter, bless the Lord! Give him glo-ry and praise for ev-er!

Verses

*Cantor:*

1. O - ceans of earth, sing glo-ry to God! Praise to the one who
2. Riv - ers and lakes, sing glo-ry to God! Praise, all you ponds and
3. Brooks of the hills, sing glo-ry to God! Praise to the source of
4. Show - ers and springs, sing glo-ry to God! Praise, all you liv - ing

formed you! Sound from your depths a hymn that tells the
bogs! Rich with the life that God cre - ates, now
life! Danc - ing with joy from peak to val - ley,
wa - ters! Show - er the earth with life and good-ness,

won - ders God has done!
let your song be heard!
laugh-ing and clear your song! Oh Bless-ed be God for
show - er the grace of God!

*All:*                                                                   D.C.

ev - er! Bless - ed be God for ev - er!

Text: Refrain trans. © 1973, ICEL; additional text by Marty Haugen, © 1994, GIA Publications, Inc.
Music: Marty Haugen, © 1994, GIA Publications, Inc.

## KYRIE ELEISON

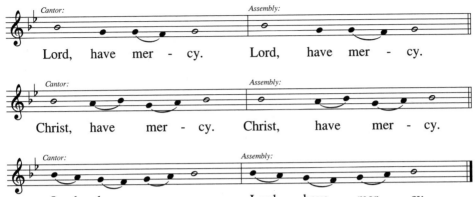

Music: Traditional chant; acc. by Richard Proulx, © 1971, GIA Publications, Inc.

*Or:*

Music: Traditional chant; acc. by Richard Proulx, © 1971, GIA Publications, Inc.

## KYRIE ELEISON

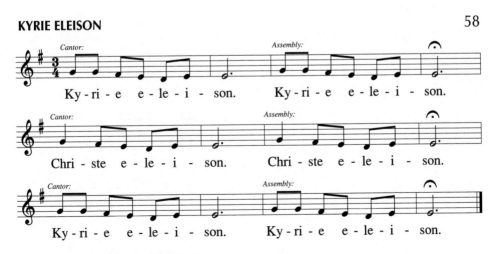

Music: *Mass of Light,* David Haas, © 1988, GIA Publications, Inc.

## 59  GLORIA (GLORY TO GOD)

Refrain

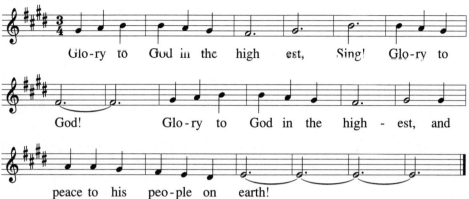

Glo-ry to God in the high - est, Sing! Glo-ry to
God! Glo-ry to God in the high - est, and
peace to his peo-ple on earth!

Verses

1. Lord God, heavenly King,
   almighty God and Father,
   we worship you, we give you thanks,
   we praise you for your glory.

2. Lord Jesus Christ, only Son of the Father,
   Lord God, Lamb of God,
   you take away the sin of the world:
   have mercy on us;
   you are seated at the right hand of the Father:
   receive our prayer.

3. For you alone are the Holy One,
   you alone are the Lord,
   the Most High, Jesus Christ,
   with the Holy Spirit,
   in the glory of God the Father.

Music: *Mass of Light,* David Haas, © 1988, GIA Publications, Inc.

## 60  HELELUYAN

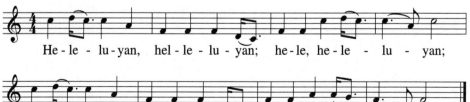

He - le - lu-yan, hel - le - lu - yan; he - le, he - le - lu - yan;
he - le - lu-yan, he - le - lu - yan; he - le, he - le - lu - yan.

Text: Traditional Muscogee Indian
Tune: Traditional Muscogee Indian; transcribed by Charles H. Webb, © 1989, The United Methodist Publishing House

## HALLE, HALLE

61

Hal - le, hal - le, hal - le - lu - jah! Hal - le, hal - le, hal -

le - lu - jah! Hal - le, hal - le, hal - le -

lu - jah! Hal - le - lu - jah! Hal - le - lu - jah!

Music: Traditional Carribean, arr. by John L. Bell, © 1990, Iona Community, GIA Publications, Inc., agent; verses and acc. by Marty Haugen, © 1993, GIA Publications, Inc.

## ALLELUIA

62

Al - le - lu - ia, al - le - lu - ia, Al - le - lu - ia, al - le - lu.

Al - le - lu - ia, al - le - lu - ia, Al - le - lu - ia, al - le - lu.

Al - le - lu - ia, al - le - lu. Al - le - lu - ia, al - le - lu.

Al - le - lu - ia, al - le - lu - ia, Al - le - lu - ia, al - le - lu.

Music: Palestinian traditional; acc. by Robert N. Roth, © 2000, GIA Publications, Inc.

## ALLELUIA

63

(Al - le - lu - ia) Al - le - lu - ia, al - le -

**D.S.**

lu - ia, al - le - lu - ia! (hum)

Music: Alleluia II, Jacques Berthier, © 1984, Les Presses de Taizé, GIA Publications, Inc., agent

## 64 HONDURAN ALLELUIA

Refrain

¡A - le - lu - ya, a - le-lu - ya! ¡A-le - lu-ya, a - le-lu - ya! ¡A - le -

lu - ya, a - le - lu - ya! ¡El Se - ñor re - su - ci-tó!

Verse

¡A - le - lu-ya! ¡A - le-lu-ya! ¡A - le-lu - ya! ¡A-le-lu-ya! ¡A-le-

lu-ya! ¡A-le-lu-ya! ¡A - le - lu - ya! ¡A - le - lu-ya! ¡A - le -

lu-ya! ¡A - le-lu - ya! ¡A - le-lu-ya! ¡A - le - lu - ya! ¡A-le-

**D.C.**

lu-ya! ¡A - le - lu - ya! ¡A - le - lu - ya! ¡A - le - lu - ya!

Psalm 150 Verses

1. Praise! Praise God in the temple, in the highest heavens!
   Praise! Praise God's mighty deeds and noble majesty!

2. Praise! Praise God with trumpet blasts, with lute and harp.
   Praise! Praise God with timbrels and dance, with strings and pipes!

3. Praise! Praise God with crashing cymbals, with ringing cymbals.
   All that is alive praise, praise the Lord.

Music: Traditional Honduran; arr. by Rob Glover, © 1997, GIA Publications, Inc.

## 65 ALLELUIA

1. *Cantor, then all:*   2.   3.

Al - le - lu - ia, al - le - lu - ia, al - le - lu - ia!

Music: *Mass of Remembrance*, Marty Haugen, © 1987, GIA Publications, Inc.

## ALLELUIA 66

Al - le-lu - ia, al - le-lu - ia! Al - le-lu - ia, al - le-lu - ia!

Al - le-lu - ia, al - le-lu - ia! Al - le-lu - ia, al - le-lu - ia!

Al - le-lu - ia, al - le-lu - ia! Al - le-lu - ia, al - le-lu - ia!

Al - le-lu-ia, al - le-lu-ia! Al - le-lu-ia, al - le-lu - ia!

Music: *Joyful Alleluia;* Howard Hughes, SM, © 1973, 1979, GIA Publications, Inc.

## ALLELUIA / LENTEN ACCLAMATION 67

Al - le - lu - ia! Al - le - lu - ia! Al - le - lu - ia!
*Lent:* Glo - ry to you, O Word of God, Lord Je - sus Christ!

Music: *Mass of Light,* David Haas, © 1988, GIA Publications, Inc.

## LENTEN ACCLAMATION 68

Praise to you, Lord Je - sus Christ, king of end-less glo-ry!

Music: Frank Schoen, © 1970, GIA Publications, Inc.

## 69 GENERAL INTERCESSIONS

Refrain

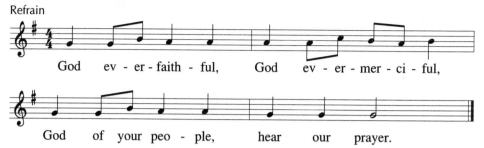

God ev - er - faith - ful, God ev - er - mer - ci - ful,

God of your peo - ple, hear our prayer.

Text: Michael Joncas
Music: Michael Joncas
© 1990, GIA Publications, Inc.

## 70 GENERAL INTERCESSIONS

*Fine*      D.C.

Ky - ri - e, Ky - ri - e, e - le - i - son. (hum)

Music: Jacques Berthier, © 1980, Les Presses de Taizé, GIA Publications, Inc., agent

## 71 CHILDREN'S ACCLAMATION 1

Ho - san - na in the high - est, ho - san - na in the high - est!

Music: Eucharistic Prayer for Children, *Mass of Creation*, Marty Haugen, adapt. by Rob Glover, © 1989, GIA Publications, Inc.

## 72 SANCTUS (HOLY, HOLY)

Ho - ly, ho - ly, ho - ly Lord, God of pow - er,

God of might, heav - en and earth are full of your

glo - ry. Ho - san - na in the high - est.

Bless - ed is he who comes in the name of the

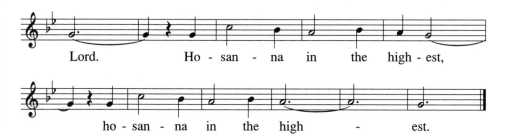

Lord. Ho - san - na in the high - est,

ho - san - na in the high - est.

Music: *Mass of Creation*, Marty Haugen, © 1984, GIA Publications, Inc.

## MEMORIAL ACCLAMATION A 73

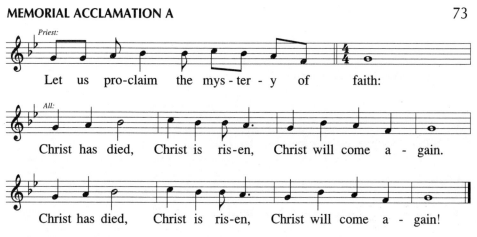

*Priest:*
Let us pro-claim the mys - ter - y of faith:

*All:*
Christ has died, Christ is ris-en, Christ will come a - gain.

Christ has died, Christ is ris-en, Christ will come a - gain!

Music: *Mass of Creation*, Marty Haugen, © 1984, GIA Publications, Inc.

## MEMORIAL ACCLAMATION B 74

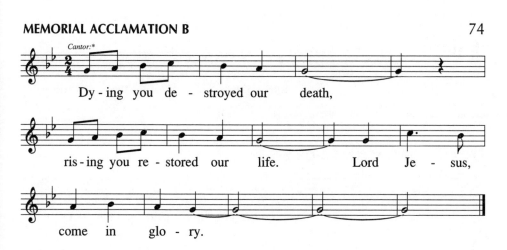

*Cantor:**
Dy - ing you de - stroyed our death,

ris - ing you re - stored our life. Lord Je - sus,

come in glo - ry.

*The assembly echoes each phrase of the cantor at the interval of one measure.

Music: *Mass of Creation*, Marty Haugen, © 1990, GIA Publications, Inc.

## 75  MEMORIAL ACCLAMATION C

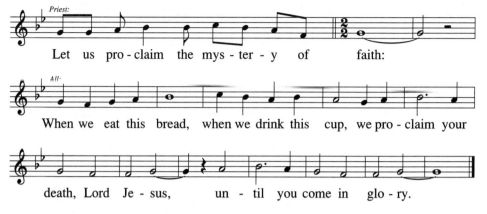

*Priest:*
Let us pro-claim the mys-ter-y of faith:

*All:*
When we eat this bread, when we drink this cup, we pro-claim your death, Lord Je-sus, un-til you come in glo-ry.

Music: *Mass of Creation,* Marty Haugen, © 1993, GIA Publications, Inc.

## 76  MEMORIAL ACCLAMATION D

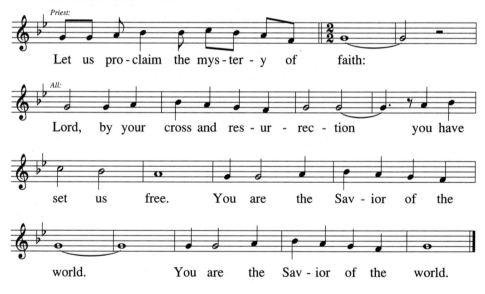

*Priest:*
Let us pro-claim the mys-ter-y of faith:

*All:*
Lord, by your cross and res-ur-rec-tion you have set us free. You are the Sav-ior of the world. You are the Sav-ior of the world.

Music: *Mass of Creation,* Marty Haugen, © 1993, GIA Publications, Inc.

## 77  CHILDREN'S ACCLAMATION 2

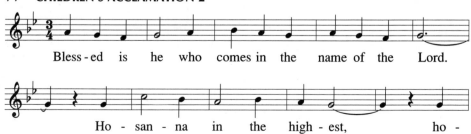

Bless-ed is he who comes in the name of the Lord.
Ho-san-na in the high-est, ho-

san - na in the high - est!

Music: Eucharistic Prayer for Children, *Mass of Creation,* Marty Haugen, adapt. by Rob Glover, © 1989, GIA Publications, Inc.

## CHILDREN'S ACCLAMATION 3            78

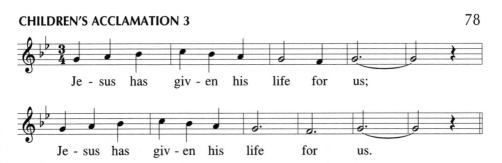

Je - sus has giv - en his life for us;

Je - sus has giv - en his life for us.

Music: Eucharistic Prayer for Children, *Mass of Creation,* Marty Haugen, adapt. by Rob Glover, © 1989, GIA Publications, Inc.

## CHILDREN'S ACCLAMATION 4            79

We praise you, we bless you, we thank you.

We praise you, we bless you, we thank you.

Music: Eucharistic Prayer for Children, *Mass of Creation,* Marty Haugen, adapt. by Rob Glover, © 1989, GIA Publications, Inc.

## AMEN            80

A - men, a - men, a - men!

A - men, a - men, a - men!

Music: *Mass of Creation,* Marty Haugen, © 1984, GIA Publications, Inc.

## 81 SANCTUS

Ho - ly, ho - ly, ho - ly Lord, God of pow - er and might, heav'n and earth are full of your glo - ry. Ho - san - na, ho - san - na, ho - san - na in the high - est. Ho - san - na, ho - san - na, ho - san - na in the high - est. Bless - ed is he who comes in the name of the Lord. Ho - san - na, ho - san - na, ho - san - na in the high - est. Ho - san - na, ho - san - na, ho - san - na in the high - est.

Music: *Mass of the Angels and Saints,* Steven R. Janco, © 1996, GIA Publications, Inc.

## 82 MEMORIAL ACCLAMATION A

Christ has died, Christ is ris - en, Christ will come a - gain.

Christ has died, Christ is ris - en, Christ will come a - gain.

Music: *Mass of the Angels and Saints,* Steven R. Janco, © 1996, GIA Publications, Inc.

## MEMORIAL ACCLAMATION B 83

Dy - ing you de - stroyed our death, ris - ing you re-stored our life.

Lord Je - sus, come in glo - ry. Lord Je - sus, come in glo - ry.

Music: *Mass of the Angels and Saints,* Steven R. Janco, © 1996, GIA Publications, Inc.

## MEMORIAL ACCLAMATION C 84

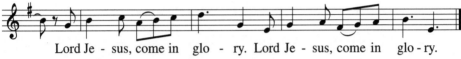

When we eat this bread, when we drink this cup, we pro-

claim your death, Lord Je - sus, un - til you come in glo - ry.

Music: *Mass of the Angels and Saints,* Steven R. Janco, © 1996, GIA Publications, Inc.

## MEMORIAL ACCLAMATION D 85

Lord, by your cross and res - ur - rec - tion you have set us free.

You are the Sav - ior of the world, the Sav - ior of the world.

Music: *Mass of the Angels and Saints,* Steven R. Janco, © 1996, GIA Publications, Inc.

## 86 CHILDREN'S ACCLAMATION 1

Je-sus has giv-en his life for us. Je-sus has giv-en his life for us.

Music: *Mass of the Angels and Saints,* Steve R. Janco, © 2000, GIA Publications, Inc.

## 87 CHILDREN'S ACCLAMATION 2

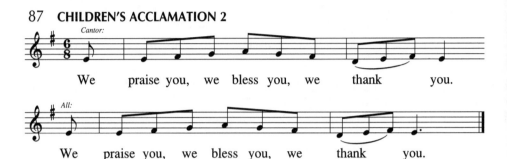

We praise you, we bless you, we thank you.

We praise you, we bless you, we thank you.

Music: *Mass of the Angels and Saints,* Steve R. Janco, © 2000, GIA Publications, Inc.

## 88 AMEN

A - men, a - men, a - men.

A - men, a - men, a - men.

Music: *Mass of the Angels and Saints,* Steven R. Janco, © 1996, GIA Publications, Inc.

## 89 HOLY, HOLY

Ho - ly, ho - ly, ho - ly Lord, God of

pow-er and might, heav-en and earth, heav-en and earth are

full of your glo - ry. Ho - sanna in the

high - est, ho - sanna in the high - est.

Bless-ed is he, bless-ed is he who comes in the name of the Lord.

Ho - san - na in the high - est, ho -

san - na in the high - est. Ho - sanna in the

high - est, ho - san - na in the high - est.

*This section may be used as an additional acclamation with the
Children's Eucharistic Prayer.

Music: *Mass of Plenty*, Rob Glover, © 2000, GIA Publications, Inc.

## MEMORIAL ACCLAMATION 90

Christ has died, Christ is ris - en, Christ will come a - gain.

Music: *Mass of Plenty*, Rob Glover, © 2000, GIA Publications, Inc.

## 91 AMEN

A - men, al - le - lu - ia, a - men, al - le - lu - ia! A - men, al - le - lu - ia, a - men, al - le - lu - ia!

Music: *Mass of Plenty,* Rob Glover, © 2000, GIA Publications, Inc.

## 92 SANCTUS

San - ctus, San - ctus, San - ctus Do - mi - nus De - us Sa - ba - oth.

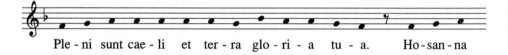

Ple - ni sunt cae - li et ter - ra glo - ri - a tu - a. Ho - san - na

in ex - cel - sis. Be - ne - di - ctus qui ve - nit in no - mi - ne

Do - mi - ni. Ho - san - na in ex - cel - sis.

Music: *Sanctus XVIII, Vatican Edition;* acc. by Gerard Farrell, OSB, © 1986, GIA Publications, Inc.

## 93 AGNUS DEI

*Cantor (first time only):*     *All:*

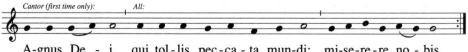

A - gnus De - i, qui tol - lis pec - ca - ta mun - di: mi - se - re - re no - bis.

A - gnus De - i, qui tol - lis pec - ca - ta mun - di: do - na no - bis pa - cem.

Music: *Agnus Dei XVIII, Vatican Edition;* acc. by Robert J. Batastini, © 1993, GIA Publications, Inc.

## AGNUS DEI (LAMB OF GOD)                                      94

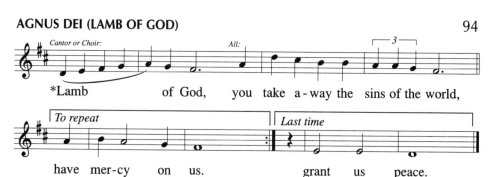

*Lamb of God, you take a-way the sins of the world,

have mer-cy on us. grant us peace.

*Alternates: 1. Emmanuel, 2. Prince of peace, 3. Son of God, 4. Word made flesh,
5. Paschal Lamb, 6. Bread of Life, 7. Lord Jesus Christ, 8. Lord of Love,
9. Christ the Lord, 10. King of kings.

Music: *Holy Cross Mass*, David Clark Isele, © 1979, GIA Publications, Inc.

## LAMB OF GOD                                                   95

1. Je - sus, Lamb of God, Bear - er of our sins,
2. Je - sus, Lamb of God, Sav - ior of the world, have
3. Je - sus, Lamb of God, Bread come down from heav'n,
4. Je - sus, Lamb of God, Shep - herd of our souls,

mer-cy on us, have mer-cy on us.

5. Je - sus, Lamb of God, gen - tle Prince of peace,

grant us peace, grant us peace.

Grant us peace, grant us peace.

Music: *Corpus Christi Mass, Adoro te devote*, setting by Richard Proulx, © 1992, GIA Publications, Inc.

## 96   LAMB OF GOD

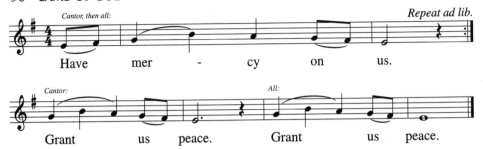

Have   mer - cy   on   us.

Grant   us   peace.   Grant   us   peace.

Music: *Mass of the Angels and Saints,* Steven R. Janco, © 1996, GIA Publications, Inc.

## 97   LAMB OF GOD

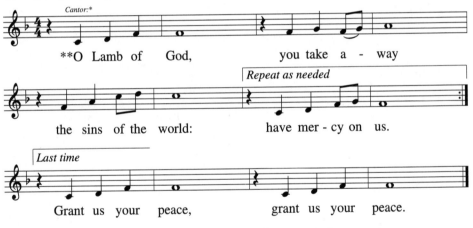

**O Lamb of   God,   you take a - way

the sins of the world:   have mer - cy on us.

Grant us your   peace,   grant us your peace.

*The assembly echoes each phrase of the cantor at the interval of one measure.*

**Additional Invocations

**Advent**
O Morning Star
O Word of God
Emmanuel

**Christmas**
O Word made flesh
Emmanuel

**Lent**
O Tree of Life

**Easter**
O Risen Lord
O Cornerstone
O Spring of Life

**General**
O Bread of Life
O Cup of Joy
O Prince of Peace

Music: Ralph R. Stewart, © 1999, GIA Publications, Inc.

# O Come, O Come, Emmanuel  98

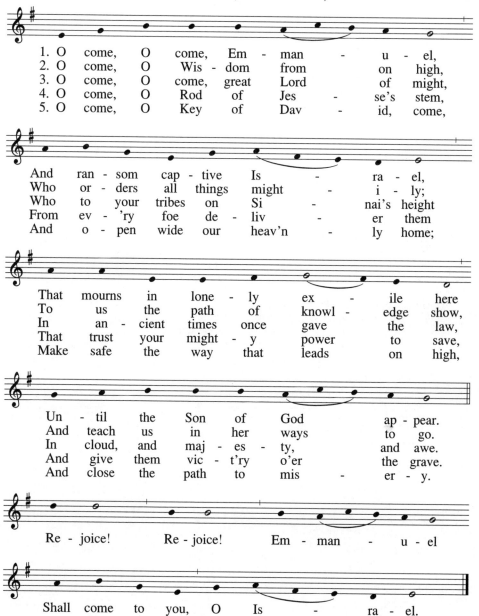

1. O come, O come, Em - man - u - el,
2. O come, O Wis - dom from on high,
3. O come, O come, great Lord of might,
4. O come, O Rod of Jes - se's stem,
5. O come, O Key of Dav - id, come,

And ran - som cap - tive Is - ra - el,
Who or - ders all things might - i - ly;
Who to your tribes on Si - nai's height
From ev - 'ry foe de - liv - er them
And o - pen wide our heav'n - ly home;

That mourns in lone - ly ex - ile here
To us the path of knowl - edge show,
In an - cient times once gave the law,
That trust your might - y power to save,
Make safe the way that leads on high,

Un - til the Son of God ap - pear.
And teach us in her ways to go.
In cloud, and maj - es - ty,
And give them vic - t'ry o'er the grave.
And close the path to mis - er - y.

Re - joice! Re - joice! Em - man - u - el

Shall come to you, O Is - ra - el.

6. O come, O Dayspring from on high
And cheer us by your drawing nigh;
Disperse the gloomy clouds of night,
And death's dark shadow put to flight.

7. O come, Desire of nations, bind
In one the hearts of humankind;
O bid our sad divisions cease,
And be for us our King of Peace.

Text: *Veni, veni Emmanuel;* Latin 9th C.; tr. by John M. Neale, 1818-1866, alt.
Tune: VENI VENI EMMANUEL, LM with refrain; Mode I; adapt. by Thomas Helmore, 1811-1890; acc. by Richard Proulx, b.1937, © 1975,
GIA Publications, Inc.

# 99 People, Look East

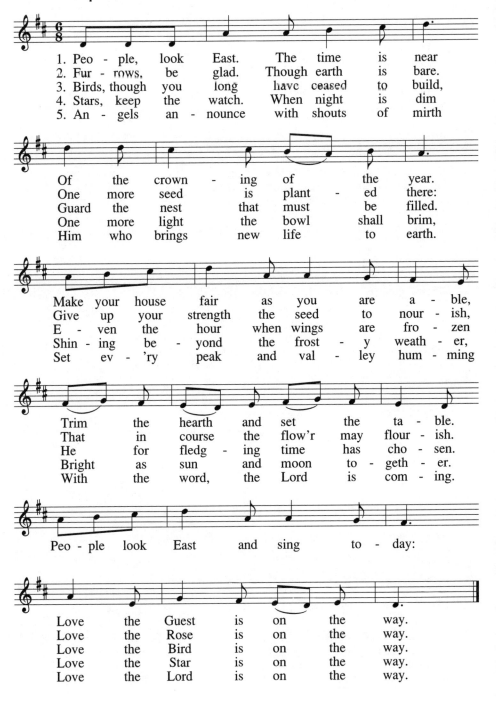

1. Peo - ple, look East. The time is near
2. Fur - rows, be glad. Though earth is bare.
3. Birds, though you long have ceased to build,
4. Stars, keep the watch. When night is dim
5. An - gels an - nounce with shouts of mirth

Of the crown - ing of the year.
One more seed is plant - ed there:
Guard the nest that must be filled.
One more light the bowl shall brim,
Him who brings new life to earth.

Make your house fair as you are a - ble,
Give up your strength the seed to nour - ish,
E - ven the hour when wings are fro - zen
Shin - ing be - yond the frost - y weath - er,
Set ev - 'ry peak and val - ley hum - ming

Trim the hearth and set the ta - ble.
That in course the flow'r may flour - ish.
He for fledg - ing time has cho - sen.
Bright as sun and moon to - geth - er.
With the word, the Lord is com - ing.

Peo - ple look East and sing to - day:

Love the Guest is on the way.
Love the Rose is on the way.
Love the Bird is on the way.
Love the Star is on the way.
Love the Lord is on the way.

Text: Eleanor Farjeon, 1881-1965, © David Higham Assoc. Ltd.
Tune: BESANCON, 87 98 87; French Traditional; harm. by Martin Shaw, 1875-1958, © Oxford University Press

# Watch for Messiah  100

1. Light one can-dle to watch for Mes - si - ah;
2. Light two can - dles to watch for Mes - si - ah;
3. Light three can - dles to watch for Mes - si - ah;
4. Light four can - dles to watch for Mes - si - ah;

Let the light ban-ish dark - ness. He shall bring sal -
Let the light ban-ish dark - ness. He shall feed his
Let the light ban-ish dark - ness. Lift your heads and
Let the light ban-ish dark - ness. He is com - ing,

va - tion to Is - ra - el, God ful - fills the prom - ise.
flock like a shep-herd, Gen - tly lead them home - ward.
lift high the gate - way, For the King of Glo - ry.
tell the glad tid - ings, Let your lights be shin - ing.

Text: Wayne L. Wold
Tune: TIF IN VELDELE, 10 7 10 6; Yiddish traditional; arr. by Wayne L. Wold
© 1984, Augsburg Fortress

# Prepare the Way of the Lord  101

Canon

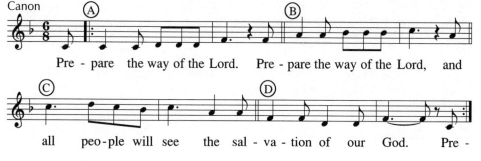

Pre - pare the way of the Lord. Pre - pare the way of the Lord, and

all peo-ple will see the sal - va - tion of our God. Pre -

Text: Luke 3:4,6; Taizé Community, 1984
Tune: Jacques Berthier, 1923-1994
© 1984, Les Presses de Taizé, GIA Publications, Inc., agent

# 102 Advent Gathering: Make Ready the Way / Come, O Lord

Cantor, then all:

Make read-y the way of the Lord! Make God a straight

path! Make read-y the way of the

Lord! Make read-y the way, make read-y the way of the Lord!

Refrain    Cantor, then all: (first time only)

Come, O Lord, change our hearts!

Em - man - u - el, God is with us.    us.

Verses    Cantor:

1. A time for hope!     Change our hearts!    A
2. Pre - pare the way!                         And
3. Come help us bring peace!                   Your

time of joy!    God is with us!
make the path straight!
king - dom come!

Text: David Haas, b.1957
Tune: David Haas, b.1957
© 1997, GIA Publications, Inc.

## Stay Awake, Be Ready 103

```
1. Stay      a - wake,        be   read - y.        You
2. Change your lives,          he's com-ing.        The
3. Change your lives,          he's com-ing.        The
4. By        the  pow'r        of the Spir - it
```

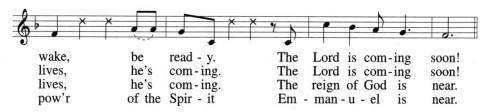

```
do   not know the hour  when the Lord  is   com-ing. Stay a -
one  who  will bap - tize with the Ho - ly   Spir - it. Change your
one  who  is   the  light of  the world is   com-ing. Change your
Mar - y    will give birth to  a   son  called Je - sus.  By  the
```

```
wake,        be   read - y.    The  Lord is com-ing   soon!
lives,       he's com-ing.     The  Lord is com-ing   soon!
lives,       he's com-ing.     The  reign of God is   near.
pow'r        of the Spir - it  Em - man - u - el is   near.
```

*If used as a Gospel Acclamation, repeat from here after the Gospel:*

```
Al - le - lu - ia, al - le - lu - ia! The  Lord is com-ing  soon!
Al - le - lu - ia, al - le - lu - ia! The  Lord is com-ing  soon!
Al - le - lu - ia, al - le - lu - ia! The  reign of God is   near.
Al - le - lu - ia, al - le - lu - ia! Em - man - u - el is   near.
```

Text: Christopher Walker, b.1947
Tune: Christopher Walker, b.1947
© 1988, 1989, 1990, Christopher Walker. Published by OCP Publications.

## Wait for the Lord 104

```
Wait    for   the Lord,    whose day  is    near.
```

```
Wait    for   the Lord:    be  strong, take  heart!
```

Text: Isaiah 40, Philippians 4, Matthew 6-7; Taizé Community, 1984
Tune: Jacques Berthier, 1923-1994
© 1984, Les Presses de Taizé, GIA Publications, Inc., agent

# 105 My Soul in Stillness Waits

**Refrain**

For you, O Lord, my soul in still - ness waits, tru - ly my hope is in you.

**Verses**

1. O Lord of Light, our on - ly hope of
2. O Spring of Joy, rain down up - on our
3. O Root of Life, im - plant your seed with -
4. O Key of Knowl - edge, guide us in our
5. Come, let us bow be - fore the God who
6. Here we shall meet the Mak - er of the

glo - ry, your ra - diance shines in all who look to
spir - its, our thirst - y hearts are yearn - ing for your
in us, and in your ad - vent, draw us all to
pil - grim-age, we ev - er seek, yet un - ful - filled re -
made us, let ev - 'ry heart be o - pened to the
heav - ens, Cre - a - tor of the moun-tains and the

you, come, light the hearts of all in dark and
Word, come, make us whole, be com - fort to our
you, our hope re - born in dy - ing and in
main, o - pen to us the path - way of your
Lord, for we are all the peo - ple of his
seas, Lord of the stars, and pres - ent to us

*D.C.*

shad - ow.
hearts.
ris - ing.
peace.
hand.
now.

Text: Psalm 95 and "O" Antiphons; Marty Haugen, b.1950
Tune: Marty Haugen, b.1950

# Joy to the World 106

1. Joy to the world! the Lord is come: Let
2. Joy to the world! the Sav - ior reigns: Let
3. He rules the world with truth and grace, And

[ꓕ]

earth re - ceive her King; Let ev - 'ry
us, our songs em - ploy; While fields and
makes the na - tions prove The glo - ries

heart pre - pare him room, And
floods, rocks, hills and plains Re -
of his right - eous - ness, And

heav'n and na - ture sing, And heav'n and na - ture
peat the sound - ing joy, Re - peat the sound - ing
won - ders of his love, And won - ders of his

sing, And heav'n, and heav'n and na - ture sing.
joy, Re - peat, re - peat the sound - ing joy.
love, And won - ders, won - ders of his love.

Text: Psalm 98; Isaac Watts, 1674-1748
Tune: ANTIOCH, CM; arr. from George F. Handel, 1685-1759, in T. Hawkes' *Collection of Tunes,* 1833

## 107 Gloria, Gloria

Canon—*4 voices*

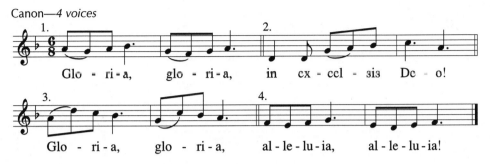

Glo - ri - a,     glo - ri - a,     in ex - cel - sis De - o!

Glo - ri - a,     glo - ri - a,     al - le - lu - ia,     al - le - lu - ia!

Tune: Jacques Berthier, 1923-1994, © 1979, 1988, Les Presses de Taizé, GIA Publications, Inc., agent

## 108 Silent Night, Holy Night

1. Si - lent night,     ho - ly night,     All     is     calm,
2. Si - lent night,     ho - ly night,     Shep - herds quake
3. Si - lent night,     ho - ly night,     Son     of     God,

all     is bright     Round yon Vir - gin Moth - er and Child,
at     the sight;     Glo - ries stream from heav - en a - far,
love's pure light     Ra - diant beams from thy ho - ly face,

Ho - ly In - fant so ten - der and mild, Sleep     in heav - en - ly
Heav'n - ly hosts sing al - le - lu - ia; Christ, the Sav - ior, is
With     the dawn of re - deem - ing grace, Je - sus, Lord, at thy

peace,     Sleep     in     heav - en - ly     peace.
born!     Christ,     the     Sav - ior,     is     born!
birth,     Je -     sus,     Lord,     at     thy     birth.

Text: *Stille Nacht, heilige Nacht;* Joseph Mohr, 1792-1849; tr. John F. Young, 1820-1885
Tune: STILLE NACHT, 66 89 66; Franz X. Gruber, 1787-1863

# Night of Silence   109

1. Cold are the peo-ple, win-ter of life, We
2. Voice in the dis-tance, call in the night, On
3. Spir-it a-mong us, shine like the star, Your

trem-ble in shad-ows this cold end-less night,
wind you en-fold us, you speak of the light,
light that guides shep-herds and kings from a-far,

Fro-zen in the snow lie ros-es sleep-ing,
Gen-tle on the ear you whis-per soft-ly,
Shim-mer in the sky so emp-ty, lone-ly,

Flow-ers that will ech-o the sun-rise,
Ru-mors of a dawn so em-brac-ing,
Ris-ing in the warmth of your Son's love,

Fire of hope is our on-ly warmth,
Breath-less love a-waits dark-ened souls,
Star un-know-ing of night and day,

Wea-ry, its flame will be dy-ing soon.
Soon will we know of the morn-ing.
Spir-it we wait for your lov-ing Son.

Text: Daniel Kantor, b.1960
Tune: Daniel Kantor, b.1960
© 1984, GIA Publications, Inc.

# 110 Away in a Manger

1. A - way in a man - ger, no crib for a bed,
2. The cat tle are low - ing; the ba - by a - wakes,
3. Be near me, Lord Je - sus; I ask you to stay

The lit - tle Lord Je - sus laid down his sweet head.
But lit - tle Lord Je - sus, no cry - ing he makes.
Close by me for - ev - er, and love me, I pray.

The stars in the bright sky looked down where he lay,
I love you, Lord Je - sus, look down from the sky,
Bless all the dear chil - dren in your ten - der care,

The lit - tle Lord Je - sus, a - sleep on the hay.
And stay by my cra - dle till morn - ing is nigh.
And fit us for heav - en to live with you there.

Text: St. 1-2, anonymous, st. 3, John T. McFarland, 1851-1913
Tune: MUELLER, 11 11 11 11; James R. Murray, 1841-1905; harm. by Robert J. Batastini, b. 1942, © 1994, GIA Publications, Inc.

# 111 He Came Down

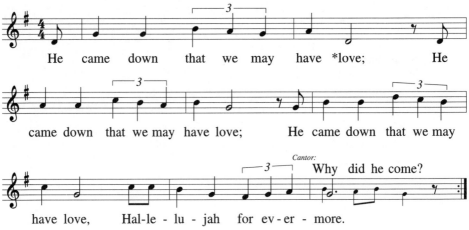

He came down that we may have *love; He

came down that we may have love; He came down that we may

Cantor: Why did he come?

have love, Hal - le - lu - jah for ev - er - more.

*Substitute peace, joy, hope, life, etc.

Text: Cameroon traditional
Tune: Cameroon traditional; transcribed and arr. by John L. Bell, b.1949, © 1990, Iona Community, GIA Publications, Inc., agent

# Angels We Have Heard on High   112

1. An - gels we have heard on high   Sweet - ly sing - ing
2. Shep-herds, why this ju - bi - lee?   Why your joy - ous
3. Come to Beth - le - hem and see   Him whose birth the
4. See him in a man - ger laid,   Whom the choirs of

o'er the plains,   And the moun - tains in re - ply
strains pro - long?   Say what may the tid - ings be,
an - gels sing;   Come a - dore, on bend - ed knee,
an - gels praise;   Mar - y, Jo - seph, lend your aid,

Ech - o back their joy - ous strains.
Which in - spire your heav'n - ly song.
Christ, the Lord, the new - born King.
While our hearts in love we raise.

Glo - - - ri - a

in ex - cel - sis De - o,   Glo - -

- - ri - a in ex-cel-sis De - o.

Text: *Les anges dans nos campagnes;* French, c. 18th C.; tr. from *Crown of Jesus Music,* London, 1862
Tune: GLORIA, 7 7 7 7 with refrain; French traditional

# 113   O Come, All Ye Faithful / Adeste Fideles

1. O come, all ye faith-ful, joy-ful and tri-um-phant, O
2. Sing, choirs of an-gels, sing in ex-ul-ta-tion,
3. Yea, Lord, we greet thee, born this hap-py morn-ing,
1. Ad-é-ste fi-dé-les, laé-ti, tri-um-phán-tes, Ve-

come ye, O come ye to Beth-le-hem;
Sing, all ye cit-i-zens of heav'n a-bove!
Je-sus, to thee be all glo-ry giv'n;
ní-te, ve-ní-te in Béth-le-hem.

Come and be-hold him, born the King of an-gels;
Glo-ry to God, all glo-ry in the high-est;
Word of the Fa-ther, now in flesh ap-pear-ing;
Na-tum vi-dé-te, Re-gem an-ge-ló-rum.

O come, let us a-dore him, O come, let us a-dore him,
Ve-ní-te a-do-ré-mus, ve-ní-te a-do-ré-mus,

O come, let us a-dore him, Christ, the Lord!
ve-ní-te a-do-ré-mus Dó-mi-num.

Text: *Adeste fideles;* John F. Wade, c.1711-1786; tr. by Frederick Oakeley, 1802-1880, alt.
Tune: ADESTE FIDELES, Irregular with refrain; John F. Wade, c.1711-1786

# 114   Go Tell It on the Mountain

Refrain

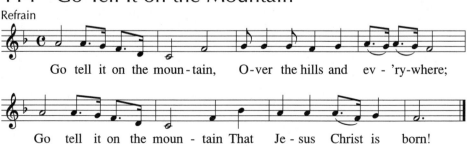

Go tell it on the moun-tain, O-ver the hills and ev-'ry-where;

Go tell it on the moun-tain That Je-sus Christ is born!

Verses

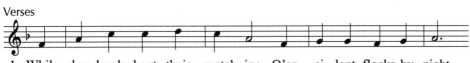

1. While shep-herds kept their watch-ing O'er si - lent flocks by night,
2. The shep-herds feared and trem-bled When lo! a - bove the earth
3. Down in a low - ly man - ger The hum-ble Christ was born,

**D.C.**

Be - hold through-out the heav-ens There shone a ho - ly light.
Rang out the an - gel cho-rus That hailed our Sav - ior's birth.
And God sent us sal - va - tion That bless - ed Christ-mas morn.

Text: African-American spiritual; adapt. by John W. Work, Jr., 1871-1925, © Mrs. John W. Work, III
Tune: GO TELL IT ON THE MOUNTAIN, 7 6 7 6 with refrain; African-American spiritual; harm. by Robert J. Batastini, b.1942, © 1995, GIA
    Publications, Inc.

## Jesus Our Brother, Kind and Good   115

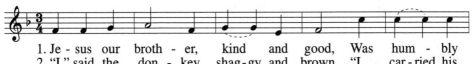

1. Je - sus our broth - er, kind and good, Was hum - bly
2. "I," said the don - key, shag-gy and brown, "I car - ried his
3. "I," said the cow, all white and red, "I gave him my

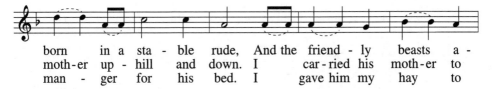

born in a sta - ble rude, And the friend - ly beasts a -
moth-er up - hill and down. I car-ried his moth-er to
man - ger for his bed. I gave him my hay to

round him stood, Je - sus our broth - er, kind and good.
Beth-le-hem town. I," said the don - key shag-gy and brown.
pil - low his head. I," said the cow all white and red.

4. "I," said the sheep with curly horn,
   "I gave him my wool for his blanket
   warm.
  He wore my coat on Christmas morn.
  I," said the sheep with curly horn.

5. "I," said the dove from rafters high,
   "I cooed him to sleep, so he should
   not cry.
  We cooed him to sleep, my mate and I.
  I," said the dove from rafters high.

6. Thus every beast by some good spell,
   in the stable dark was glad to tell
   of the gift he gave Emmanuel,
   the gift he gave Emmanuel.

Text: Traditional English carol
Tune: ORIENTIS PARTIBUS, 8 9 9 8; Pierre de Corbiel, d.1222; harm. by Margaret Mealy, b.1922, © 1961, General Convention of the Episcopal
   Church, USA

## 116   The Virgin Mary Had a Baby Boy

1. The vir - gin Mar - y had a ba - by boy, the
2. The an - gels sang when the ba - by born, the
3. The wise men saw where the ba - by born, the

vir - gin Mar - y had a ba - by boy, the
an - gels sang when the ba - by born, the
wise men saw where the ba - by born, the

vir - gin Mar - y had a ba - by boy, and they
an - gels sang when the ba - by born, and they
wise men went where the ba - by born, and they

say that his name was Je - sus.
say that his name was Je - sus.
say that his name was Je - sus.

He come from the glo - ry, he come from the

glo - rious king - dom. Oh, yes! be - liev - er!

Oh, yes! be - liev - er! He come from the

glo - ry, he come from the glo - rious king-dom.

Text: West Indian carol, © 1945, Boosey and Co., Ltd.
Tune: West Indian carol, © 1945, Boosey and Co., Ltd.; acc. by Robert J. Batastini, b.1942, © 1993, GIA Publications, Inc.

"To those who love God, all things work together
for good ..." Romans 8:28

24

30

35

**STUDENT
ESSAY
CONTEST
$1,000**

See theme and rules on page 9

9

# We Three Kings of Orient Are 117

1. We three kings of O - ri - ent are, Bear - ing
2. Born a babe on Beth - le - hem's plain, Gold we
3. Frank - in - cense to of - fer have I; In - cense
4. Myrrh is mine: its bit - ter per - fume Breathes a
5. Glo - rious now be - hold him rise, King and

gifts we trav - erse a - far Field and foun - tain,
bring to crown him a - gain; King for - ev - er,
owns a De - i - ty nigh, Prayer and prais - ing
life of gath - 'ring gloom; Sor - rowing, sigh - ing,
God and sac - ri - fice: Heav'n sings, "Hal - le -

Moor and moun - tain, Fol - low - ing yon - der star.
Ceas - ing nev - er, O - ver us all to reign.
Glad - ly rais - ing, Wor - ship - ing God on high.
Bleed - ing, dy - ing, Sealed in the stone cold tomb.
lu - jah!" "Hal - le - lu - jah!" earth re - plies.

O star of won - der, star of night, Star with

roy - al beau - ty bright, West - ward lead - ing, still pro -

ceed - ing, Guide us to the per - fect Light.

Text: Matthew 2:1-11; John H. Hopkins, Jr., 1820-1891
Tune: KINGS OF ORIENT, 88 44 6 with refrain; John H. Hopkins, Jr., 1820-1891

## 118 O Come, Little Children

1. O come, lit-tle chil-dren, O come, one and all. O
2. The hay is his pil-low, the man-ger his bed. The
3. O bow with the shep-herds on low bend-ed knee, With

come to the cra-dle in Beth-le-hem's stall. Come
beasts stand in won-der to gaze on his head. Yet
hearts full of thanks for the gift which you see. Come,

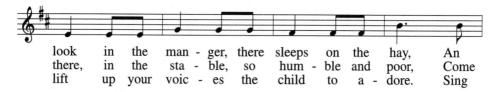

look in the man-ger, there sleeps on the hay, An
there, in the sta-ble, so hum-ble and poor, Come
lift up your voic-es the child to a-dore. Sing

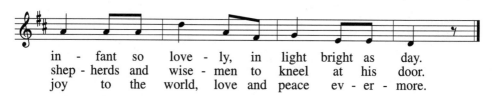

in-fant so love-ly, in light bright as day.
shep-herds and wise-men to kneel at his door.
joy to the world, love and peace ev-er-more.

Text: Christian von Schmidt, 1768-1854; trans. unknown
Tune: IHR KINDERLEIN KOMMET, 11 11 11 11; Johann Abraham Peter Schulz, 1747-1800; acc. by Robert N. Roth, © 2000, GIA Publications, Inc.

## 119 What Star Is This

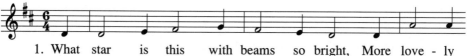

1. What star is this with beams so bright, More love-ly
2. 'Tis now ful-filled what God de-creed, "From Ja-cob
3. O Je-sus, while the star of grace Im-pels us
4. To God Cre-a-tor, heav'n-ly light, To Christ, re-

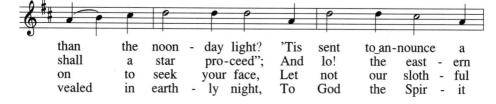

than the noon-day light? 'Tis sent to an-nounce a
shall a star pro-ceed"; And lo! the east-ern
on to seek your face, Let not our sloth-ful
vealed in earth-ly night, To God the Spir-it

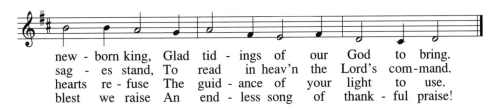

new - born king, Glad tid - ings of our God to bring.
sag - es stand, To read in heav'n the Lord's com-mand.
hearts re - fuse The guid - ance of your light to use.
blest we raise An end - less song of thank - ful praise!

Text: *Quem stella sole pulchrior,* Charles Coffin, 1676-1749; tr. by John Chandler, 1806-1876, alt.
Tune: PUER NOBIS, LM; adapt. by Michael Praetorius, 1571-1621

## Dust and Ashes 120

Verses

1. Dust and ash - es touch our face, mark our fail - ure and our
2. Dust and ash - es soil our hands— greed of mar - ket, pride of
3. Dust and ash - es choke our tongue in the waste-land of de -

fall - ing. Ho - ly Spir - it, come, walk with us to - mor - row,
na - tion. Ho - ly Spir - it, come, walk with us to - mor - row,
pres-sion. Ho - ly Spir - it, come, walk with us to - mor - row,

take us as dis - ci - ples, washed and wak-ened by your call-ing.
as we pray and strug-gle through the mesh - es of op - pres-sion.
through all gloom and griev-ing to the paths of res - ur - rec - tion.

Refrain

Take us by the hand and lead us, lead us through the des - ert sands,

bring us liv - ing wa - ter, Ho - ly Spir - it, come.

Text: Brian Wren, b.1936, © 1989, Hope Publishing Co.
Tune: David Haas, b.1957, © 1991, GIA Publications, Inc.

# 121 Again We Keep This Solemn Fast

1. Again we keep this solemn fast
   A gift of faith from ages past,
   This Lent which binds us lovingly
   To faith and hope and charity.

2. The law and prophets from of old
   In figured ways this Lent foretold,
   Which Christ, all ages' Lord and Guide,
   In these last days has sanctified.

3. More sparing, therefore, let us make
   The words we speak, the food we take,
   Our sleep, our laughter, ev'ry sense;
   Learn peace through holy penitence.

4. Let us avoid each harmful way
   That lures the careless mind astray;
   By watchful prayer our spirits free
   From scheming of the Enemy.

5. We pray, O blessed Three in One,
   Our God while endless ages run,
   That this, our Lent of forty days,
   May bring us growth and give you praise.

Text: *Ex more docti mystico;* ascr. to Gregory the Great, c. 540-604, tr. by Peter J. Scagnelli, b. 1949, ©
Tune: OLD HUNDREDTH, LM; Louis Bourgeois, c.1510-1561

# 122 Jesus, Remember Me

**Ostinato Refrain**

Jesus, remember me when you come into your Kingdom.

Jesus, remember me when you come into your Kingdom.

Text: Luke 23:42; Taizé Community, 1981
Tune: Jacques Berthier, 1923-1994
© 1981, Les Presses de Taizé, GIA Publications, Inc., agent

# O Sun of Justice  123

1. O Sun of jus-tice, Je - sus Christ, Dis - pel the
2. In this our "time ac - cept - a - ble" Touch ev - 'ry
3. The day, your day, in beau - ty dawns When in your
4. O lov - ing Trin - i - ty, our God, To you we

dark - ness of our hearts, Till your blest light makes
heart with sor - row, Lord, That, turned from sin, re -
light earth blooms a - new; Led back a - gain to
bow through end - less days, And in your grace new -

night - time flee And brings the joys your day im - parts.
newed by grace, We may press on toward love's re - ward.
life's true way, May we, for - giv'n, re - joice in you.
born we sing New hymns of grat - i - tude and praise.

Text: *Jam Christe sol justitiae;* Latin, 6th C.; tr. by Peter J. Scagnelli, b.1949, ©
Tune: JESU DULCIS MEMORIA, LM; Mode I; acc. by Richard Proulx, b.1937, © 1975, GIA Publications, Inc.

# O How Good is Christ the Lord  124

O how good is Christ the Lord! On the cross he died for me.

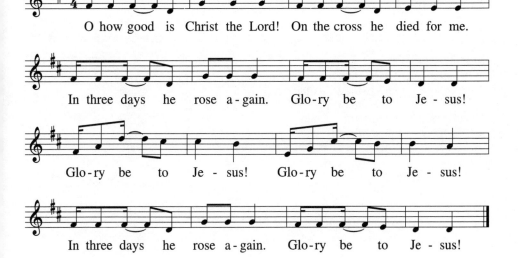

In three days he rose a - gain. Glo-ry be to Je - sus!

Glo-ry be to Je - sus! Glo-ry be to Je - sus!

In three days he rose a - gain. Glo-ry be to Je - sus!

Text: Puerto Rican traditional
Tune: OH QUE BUENO ES JESUS, 7 7 7 6 6 6 7 6; Puerto Rican traditional; acc. by Robert J. Batastini, b.1942, © 2000, GIA Publications, Inc.

## 125  Were You There

1. Were you there when they cru - ci - fied my Lord?
2. Were you there when they nailed him to the tree?
3. Were you there when they pierced him in the side?
4. Were you there when the sun re - fused to shine?
5. Were you there when they laid him in the tomb?
6. Were you there when they rolled the stone a - way?

Were you there when they cru - ci - fied my Lord?
Were you there when they nailed him to the tree?
Were you there when they pierced him in the side?
Were you there when the sun re - fused to shine?
Were you there when they laid him in the tomb?
Were you there when they rolled the stone a - way?

Oh! Some - times it caus - es me to

trem - ble, trem - ble, trem - ble, Were you

there when they cru - ci - fied my Lord?
there when they nailed him to the tree?
there when they pierced him in the side?
there when the sun re - fused to shine?
there when they laid him in the tomb?
there when they rolled the stone a - way?

Text: African-American spiritual
Tune: WERE YOU THERE, 10 10 with refrain; African-American spiritual; harm. by Robert J. Batastini, b.1942, © 1987, GIA Publications, Inc.

# What Wondrous Love Is This   126

1. What won-drous love is this, O my soul, O my soul?
2. To God and to the Lamb I will sing, I will sing;
3. And when from death I'm free, I'll sing on, I'll sing on;

What won-drous love is this, O my soul?
To God and to the Lamb, I will sing;
And when from death I'm free, I'll sing on;

What won-drous love is this that caused the Lord of bliss
To God and to the Lamb who is the great I Am,
And when from death I'm free, I'll sing and joy-ful be,

To bear the dread-ful curse for my soul, for my soul;
While mil-lions join the theme, I will sing, I will sing;
And through e-ter-ni-ty I'll sing on, I'll sing on!

To bear the dread-ful curse for my soul?
While mil-lions join the theme, I will sing.
And through e-ter-ni-ty I'll sing on.

Text: Alexander Means, 1801-1853
Tune: WONDROUS LOVE, 12 9 12 12 9; *Southern Harmony*, 1835; harm. from *Cantate Domino, 1980*, © 1980, World Council of Churches

## 127 Lead Me, Guide Me

**Refrain**

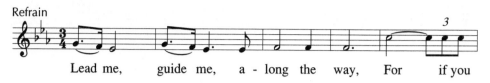

Lead me, guide me, a - long the way, For if you

lead me, I can-not stray. Lord, let me walk each

day with thee. Lead me, oh Lord, lead me.

**Verses**

1. I am weak and I need thy strength and pow'r to
2. Help me tread in the paths of right - eous - ness, Be my
3. I am lost if you take your hand from me, I am

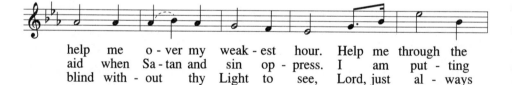

help me o - ver my weak - est hour. Help me through the
aid when Sa - tan and sin op - press. I am put - ting
blind with - out thy Light to see, Lord, just al - ways

**D.C.**

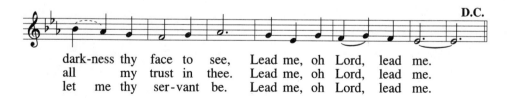

dark-ness thy face to see, Lead me, oh Lord, lead me.
all my trust in thee. Lead me, oh Lord, lead me.
let me thy ser-vant be. Lead me, oh Lord, lead me.

Text: Doris M. Akers, b.1922
Tune: Doris M. Akers, b.1922, harm. by Richard Smallwood
© 1953, Doris M. Akers, All rights administered by Unichappell Music, Inc.

# Now We Remain 128

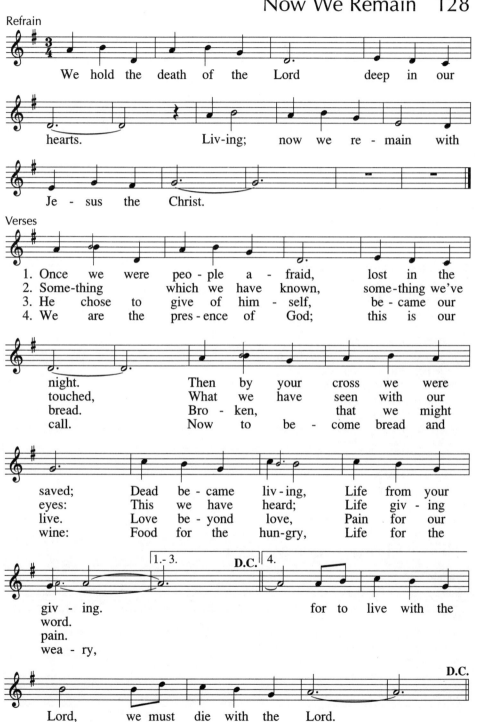

**Refrain**

We hold the death of the Lord deep in our hearts. Liv-ing; now we re - main with Je - sus the Christ.

**Verses**

1. Once we were peo - ple a - fraid, lost in the night. Then by your cross we were saved; Dead be - came liv - ing, Life from your giv - ing.

2. Some-thing which we have known, some-thing we've touched, What we have seen with our eyes: This we have heard; Life giv - ing word.

3. He chose to give of him - self, be - came our bread. Bro - ken, that we might live. Love be - yond love, Pain for our pain.

4. We are the pres - ence of God; this is our call. Now to be - come bread and wine: Food for the hun-gry, Life for the wea - ry,

[1.-3.] giv - ing. word. pain.

**D.C.**

[4.] wea - ry, for to live with the Lord, we must die with the Lord.

**D.C.**

Text: Corinthians, 1 John, 2 Timothy; David Haas, b.1957
Tune: David Haas, b.1957

## 129 Return to God

Refrain

Re - turn to God with all your heart, the source of grace and mer - cy; come seek the ten - der faith - ful - ness of God.

Verses

1. Now the time of grace has come,
   the day of salvation;
   come and learn now the way of our God.

2. I will take your heart of stone
   and place a heart within you,
   a heart of compassion and love.

3. If you break the chains of oppression,
   if you set the pris'ner free;
   if you share your bread with the hungry,
   give protection to the lost;
   give a shelter to the homeless,
   clothe the naked in your midst,
   then your light shall break forth like the dawn.

Text: Marty Haugen, b.1950
Tune: Marty Haugen, b.1950
© 1990, 1991, GIA Publications, Inc.

## 130 O Lord, Hear My Prayer

Ostinato Chorale

O Lord, hear my prayer, O Lord, hear my prayer:
*The Lord is my song, the Lord is my praise:

when I call an - swer me. O Lord, hear my prayer, O
all my hope comes from God. The Lord is my song, the

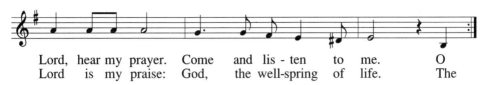

Lord, hear my prayer. Come and lis-ten to me. O
Lord is my praise: God, the well-spring of life. The

*Alternate text

Text: Psalm 102; Taizé Community, 1982
Tune: Jacques Berthier, 1923-1994
© 1982, Les Presses de Taizé, GIA Publications, Inc., agent

## Christ the Lord Is Risen! 131

1. Christ the Lord is ris'n! Christ the Lord is ris'n!
2. He has con-quered death. He has con-quered death.
3. Sin has done its worst. Sin has done its worst.
4. He is King of kings. He is King of kings.
5. He is Lord of lords. He is Lord of lords.
6. All the world is his. All the world is his.
7. Come and wor-ship him. Come and wor-ship him.
8. Christ our Lord is ris'n! Christ our Lord is ris'n!
9. Hal-le-lu - jah! Hal-le-lu - jah!

Je - su. Christ the Lord is ris'n!
Je - su. He has con - quered death.
Je - su. Sin has done its worst.
Je - su. He is King of kings.
Je - su. He is Lord of lords.
Je - su. All the world is his.
Je - su. Come and wor - ship him.
Je - su. Christ our Lord is ris'n!
Je - su. Hal - le - lu - jah!

Christ the Lord is ris'n! Je - su.
He has con - quered death. Je - su.
Sin has done its worst. Je - su.
He is King of kings. Je - su.
He is Lord of lords. Je - su.
All the world is his. Je - su.
Come and wor - ship him. Je - su.
Christ our Lord is ris'n! Je - su.
Hal - le - lu - jah! Je - su.

Text: Tom Colvin, b.1925
Tune: GARU, 55 2 55 2; Ghanian folk song, adapt. by Tom Colvin, b.1925, arr. by Kevin R. Hackett
© 1969, Hope Publishing Company

## 132 Alleluia, Alleluia, Give Thanks

Refrain

Al - le - lu - ia, al - le - lu - ia, give thanks to the ris - en Lord.

Al - le - lu - ia, al - le - lu - ia, give praise to his Name.

Verses

1. Je - sus is Lord of all the earth.
2. Spread the good news o'er all the earth:
3. We have been cru - ci - fied with Christ.
4. God has pro - claimed his gra - cious gift:
5. Come, let us praise the liv - ing God,

D.C.

He is the King of cre - a - tion.
Je - sus has died and has ris - en.
Now we shall live for ev - er.
Life e - ter - nal for all who be - lieve.
Joy - ful - ly sing to our Sav - ior.

Text: Donald Fishel, b.1950
Tune: ALLELUIA NO. 1, 8 8 with refrain; Donald Fishel, b.1950
© 1973, Word of God Music

## 133 Surrexit Christus / The Lord Is Risen

Ostinato Refrain

*(hum)*     Sur - re - xit Chri - stus, al - le - lu - ia!
*The Lord is ris - en, al - le - lu - ia!*

*(hum)*     Can - ta - te Do - mi - no, al - le - lu - ia!
*Sing out and praise the Lord, al - le - lu - ia!*

Text: *Christ is risen, sing to the Lord;* Daniel 3; Taizé Community, 1984
Tune: Jacques Berthier, 1923-1994
© 1984, Les Presses de Taizé, GIA Publications, Inc., agent

# Jubilate Servite / Raise a Song of Gladness  134

*Canon—2 voices*

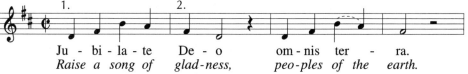

Ju - bi - la - te   De - o   om - nis ter - ra.
*Raise a song of   glad-ness,   peo-ples of the   earth.*

Ser - vi - te   Do - mi - no   in lae - ti - ti - a.
*Christ has come,   bring-ing peace,   joy to ev-'ry heart.*

Al - le - lu - ia,   al - le - lu - ia,   in lae - ti - ti - a!
*Al - le - lu - ia,   al - le - lu - ia,   joy to ev -'ry heart!*

Al - le - lu - ia,   al - le - lu - ia,   in lae - ti - ti - a!
*Al - le - lu - ia,   al - le - lu - ia,   joy to ev -'ry heart!*

Text: Psalm 100, *Rejoice in God, all the earth, Serve the Lord with gladness;* Taizé Community, 1978
Tune: Jacques Berthier, 1923-1994
© 1979, Les Presses de Taizé, GIA Publications, Inc., agent

# Jubilate Deo / In the Lord Rejoicing  135

*Canon*

Ⓐ   Ⓑ   Ⓒ
Ju - bi - la - te De - o,   ju - bi - la - te
*In   the   Lord re - joic - ing!   Christ is ris - en*

Ⓓ   Ⓔ
De - o,   al - le - lu - ia!
*from the dead!   Al - le - lu - ia!*

Text: Psalm 100:1; tr. Taizé Community, 1990, © 1978, 1990, Les Presses de Taizé, GIA Publications, Inc., agent
Tune: Michael Praetorius, 1571-1621; acc. by Jacques Berthier, 1923-1994, © 1978, 1990, Les Presses de Taizé, GIA Publications, Inc., agent

# 136 People of God / Alleluia

Verses

1. New be - gin - nings, here in our midst:
2. Called to al - ways live in the light:
3. We are now sons and daugh - ters of God:
4. Called to go forth to love and serve:

Al -

le - lu-ia! Al - le - lu-ia!

We are God's chil - dren,
Called to be signs of God's
To - geth - er to live as the
Build - ing the king - dom of

ho - ly and blest:
won - der - ful love:
Bod - y of Christ:
jus - tice and peace:

Al - le - lu - ia! Al - le - lu - ia!

Peo - ple of God, re - joice and sing!

Refrain

Al - le - lu - ia! Al - le - lu - ia!

Al - le - lu - ia! Al - le - lu - ia!

Text: David Haas, b.1957
Tune: Refrain by Fintan O'Carroll; verses by David Haas, b.1957
© 1982, 1991, 1997, GIA Publications, Inc.

# Easter Alleluia  137

Refrain

Al-le-lu-ia, al - le - lu-ia, al-le-lu - ia!

Verses

1. Glo - ry to God who does won - drous things, Let all the
2. See how sal - va - tion for all has been won, Up from the
3. Now in our pres - ence the Lord will ap - pear, Shine in the
4. Call us, Good Shep - herd, we lis - ten for you, Want-ing to
5. Lord, we are o - pen to all that you say, Read - y to
6. If we have love, then we dwell in the Lord, God will pro -

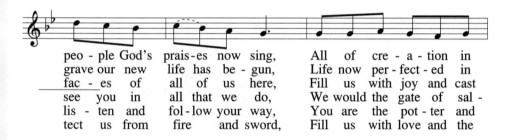

peo - ple God's prais-es now sing, All of cre - a - tion in
grave our new life has be - gun, Life now per - fect - ed in
fac - es of all of us here, Fill us with joy and cast
see you in all that we do, We would the gate of sal -
lis - ten and fol-low your way, You are the pot - ter and
tect us from fire and sword, Fill us with love and the

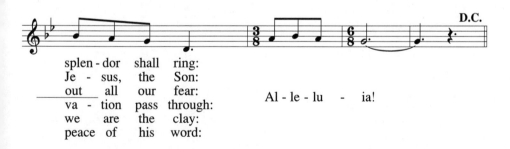

D.C.

splen - dor shall ring:
Je - sus, the Son:
out all our fear:          Al - le - lu - ia!
va - tion pass through:
we are the clay:
peace of his word:

Text: Marty Haugen, b.1950
Tune: O FILII ET FILIAE; 10 10 10 with alleluias, adapt. by Marty Haugen, b.1950
© 1986, GIA Publications, Inc.

# 138 This Day Was Made by the Lord

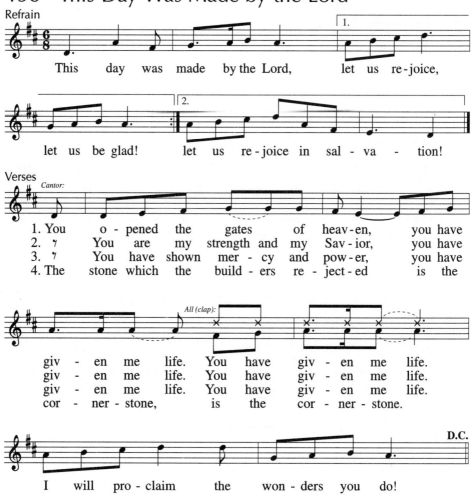

**Refrain**

This day was made by the Lord, let us re-joice,

let us be glad! let us re-joice in sal - va - tion!

**Verses**

*Cantor:*

1. You o - pened the gates of heav-en, you have
2. ⁊ You are my strength and my Sav - ior, you have
3. ⁊ You have shown mer - cy and pow-er, you have
4. The stone which the build - ers re - ject-ed is the

*All (clap):*

giv - en me life. You have giv - en me life.
giv - en me life. You have giv - en me life.
giv - en me life. You have giv - en me life.
cor - ner - stone, is the cor - ner - stone.

I will pro - claim the won - ders you do!

Text: Christopher Walker, b.1947
Tune: Christopher Walker, b.1947
© 1988, 1989, Christopher Walker. Published by OCP Publications.

# 139 Sing a New Song

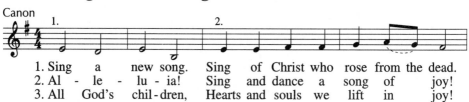

**Canon**

1. Sing a new song. Sing of Christ who rose from the dead.
2. Al - le - lu - ia! Sing and dance a song of joy!
3. All God's chil-dren, Hearts and souls we lift in joy!

| Al - le-lu - ia! Al - le-lu - ia! | Sing a new song. |
| Christ now lives a - mong us. | Al - le-lu - ia! |
| Give thanks to the Lord as | Chil - dren of God. |

Text: Robert Piercy, © 2001, GIA Publications, Inc.
Tune: Thomas Ravenscroft, c.1582-1635; acc. by Robert N. Roth, © 2000, GIA Publications, Inc.

## Jesus Christ Is Risen Today  140

1. Je - sus Christ is ris'n to - day, Al - le - lu - ia!
2. Hymns of praise then let us sing, Al - le - lu - ia!
3. But the pains which he en - dured, Al - le - lu - ia!
4. Sing we to our God a - bove, Al - le - lu - ia!

Our tri - um-phant ho - ly day, Al - le - lu - ia!
Un - to Christ, our heav'n-ly King, Al - le - lu - ia!
Our sal - va - tion have pro - cured; Al - le - lu - ia!
Praise e - ter - nal as his love; Al - le - lu - ia!

Who did once up - on the cross, Al - le - lu - ia!
Who en - dured the cross and grave, Al - le - lu - ia!
Now a - bove the sky he's King, Al - le - lu - ia!
Praise him, now his might con - fess, Al - le - lu - ia!

Suf - fer to re - deem our loss. Al - le - lu - ia!
Sin - ners to re - deem and save. Al - le - lu - ia!
Where the an - gels ev - er sing. Al - le - lu - ia!
Fa - ther, Son, and Spir - it blest. Al - le - lu - ia!

Text: St. 1, *Surrexit Christus hodie*, Latin, 14th C.; para. in *Lyra Davidica*, 1708, alt.; st. 2, 3, *The Compleat Psalmodist*, c.1750, alt.; st. 4, Charles
Wesley, 1707-1788
Tune: EASTER HYMN, 77 77 with alleluias; *Lyra Davidica*, 1708

## 141 Christ the Lord Is Risen Today / Hail the Day That Sees Him Rise

Text: Charles Wesley, 1707-1788
Tune: LLANFAIR, 77 77 with alleluias; Robert Williams, 1781-1821

# Alleluia! Sing to Jesus · 142

1. Al - le - lu - ia! sing to Je - sus! His the
2. Al - le - lu - ia! not as or - phans Are we
3. Al - le - lu - ia! Bread of An - gels, Here on
4. Al - le - lu - ia! King e - ter - nal, You the

scep - ter, his the throne; Al - le - lu - ia!
left in sor - row now; Al - le - lu - ia!
earth our food, our stay! Al - le - lu - ia!
Lord of lords we own; Al - le - lu - ia!

his the tri - umph, His the vic - to - ry a - lone;
he is near us, Faith be - lieves, nor ques - tions how:
here the sin - ful Flee to you from day to day:
born of Mar - y, Earth your foot - stool, heav'n your throne:

Hark! the songs of peace - ful Zi - on Thun - der
Though the cloud from sight re - ceived him, When the
In - ter - ces - sor, friend of sin - ners, Earth's re -
You, with - in the veil, have en - tered, Robed in

like a might - y flood; Je - sus out of
for - ty days were o'er, Shall our hearts for -
deem - er, plead for me, Where the songs of
flesh, our great high priest; Here on earth both

ev - 'ry na - tion Has re - deemed us by his blood.
get his prom - ise, "I am with you ev - er - more"?
all the sin - less Sweep a - cross the crys - tal sea.
priest and vic - tim In the eu - cha - ris - tic feast.

Text: Revelation 5:9; William C. Dix, 1837-1898
Tune: HYFRYDOL, 8 7 8 7 D; Rowland H. Prichard, 1811-1887

## 143 That Easter Day with Joy Was Bright

1. That Eas - ter day with joy was bright,
2. His ris - en flesh with ra - diance glowed;
3. O Je - sus, King of gen - tle - ness,
4. O Lord of all, with us a - bide
5. All praise, to you, O ris - en Lord,

The sun shone out with fair - er light,
His wound - ed hands and feet he showed;
Who with your grace our hearts pos - sess
In this our joy - ful East - er - tide;
Now both by heav'n and earth a - dored;

When to their long - ing eyes re - stored,
Those scars their sol - emn wit - ness gave
That we may give you all our days
From ev - 'ry weap - on death can wield
To God the Fa - ther e - qual praise,

The a - pos - tles saw their ris - en Lord.
That Christ was ris - en from the grave.
The will - ing trib - ute of our praise.
Your own re - deemed for ev - er shield.
And Spir - it blest, our songs we raise.

Text: *Claro paschali gaudio;* Latin 5th C.; tr. by John M. Neale, 1818-1866, alt.
Tune: PUER NOBIS, LM; adapt. by Michael Praetorius, 1571-1621

## 144 All Creatures of Our God and King

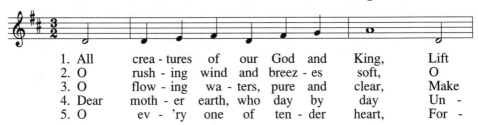

1. All crea - tures of our God and King, Lift
2. O rush - ing wind and breez - es soft, O
3. O flow - ing wa - ters, pure and clear, Make
4. Dear moth - er earth, who day by day Un -
5. O ev - 'ry one of ten - der heart, For -

up your voice and with us sing: Al - le - lu - ia! Al - le -
clouds that ride the winds a - loft: Al - le - lu - ia! Al - le -
mu - sic for your Lord to hear. Al - le - lu - ia! Al - le -
folds rich bless - ings on our way, Al - le - lu - ia! Al - le -
giv - ing oth - ers, take your part, Al - le - lu - ia! Al - le -

lu - ia! O burn - ing sun with gold - en beam And
lu - ia! O ris - ing morn, in praise re - joice, O
lu - ia! O fire so mas - ter - ful and bright, Pro -
lu - ia! The fruits and flow'rs that ver - dant grow, Let
lu - ia! All you who pain and sor - row bear, Praise

sil - ver moon with soft - er gleam:
lights of eve - ning, find a voice.
vid - ing us with warmth and light, Al - le -
them God's glo - ry al - so show.
God and cast on God your care.

lu - ia! Al - le - lu - ia! Al - le - lu - ia, al - le -

lu - ia, al - le - lu - ia!

6. And you, most kind and gentle death,
   Waiting to hush our final breath,
   Alleluia! Alleluia!
   You lead to heav'n the child of God,
   Where Christ our Lord the way has trod.
   Alleluia! Alleluia!
   Alleluia, alleluia, alleluia!

7. Let all things their Creator bless,
   And worship God in humbleness,
   Alleluia! Alleluia!
   Oh praise the Father, praise the Son,
   And praise the Spirit, Three in One!
   Alleluia! Alleluia!
   Alleluia, alleluia, alleluia!

Text: *Laudato si, mi Signor;* Francis of Assisi, 1182-1226; tr. by William H. Draper, 1855-1933, alt., © J. Curwen and Sons
Tune: LASST UNS ERFREUEN, LM with alleluias; *Geistliche Kirchengesänge,* 1623; harm. by Ralph Vaughan Williams, 1872-1958, © Oxford
  University Press

# 145 Canticle of the Sun

**Refrain**

The heav-ens are tell-ing the glo-ry of God,
and all cre-a-tion is shout-ing for joy. Come,
dance in the for-est, come, play in the field, and
sing, sing to the glo-ry of the Lord.

**Verses**

1. Praise for the sun, the bring-er of day, He car-ries the
2. Praise for the wind that blows through the trees, The seas might-y
3. Praise for the rain that wa-ters our fields, And bless-es our
4. Praise for the fire who gives us his light, The warmth of the
5. Praise for the earth who makes life to grow, The crea-tures you
6. Praise for our death that makes our life real, The knowl-edge of

light of the Lord in his rays; The moon and the stars who
storms, the gen-tl-est breeze; They blow where they will, they
crops so all the earth yields; From death un-to life her
sun to bright-en our night; He danc-es with joy, his
made to let your life show; The flow-ers and trees that
loss that helps us to feel; The gift of your-self, your

*D.C.*

light up the way Un-to your throne.
blow where they please To please the Lord.
mys-t'ry re-vealed Springs forth in joy.
spir-it so bright, He sings of you.
help us to know The heart of love.
pres-ence re-vealed To lead us home.

Text: Marty Haugen, b.1950
Tune: Marty Haugen, b.1950
© 1980, GIA Publications, Inc.

# All People That on Earth Do Dwell   146

1. All peo - ple that on earth do dwell,
2. Know that there is one God, in - deed,
3. En - ter the sa - cred gates with praise,
4. Pro - claim a - gain that God is good,
5. To Fa - ther, Son, and Ho - ly Ghost,
* Praise God, from whom all bless - ings flow;
†*Praise God, from whom all bless - ings flow.*

Sing out your faith with cheer - ful voice;
Who fash - ions us with - out our aid,
With joy ap - proach the tem - ple walls.
Whose mer - cy is for - ev - er sure,
The God whom heav'n and earth a - dore,
Praise him, all crea - tures here be - low;
*Praise God, all crea - tures here be - low.*

De - light in God whose praise you tell,
Who claims us, gives us all we need,
Ex - tol and bless our God al - ways
Whose truth at all times firm - ly stood,
From us and from the an - gel host
Praise him a - bove, you heav'n - ly host:
*Cre - a - tor, Sav - ior, Spir - it, praise,*

Whose pres - ence calls you to re - joice.
Whose ten - der care will nev - er fade.
As peo - ple whom the Spir - it calls.
And shall from age to age en - dure.
Be praise and glo - ry ev - er - more.
Praise Fa - ther, Son and Ho - ly Ghost.
*In joy - ful song through all our days.*

\* *May be sung alone or as an alternate to stanza 5.*
†*Alternate version of \* verse.*

Text: Psalm (99)100; William Kethe, d. c.1593, alt.; Doxology, Thomas Ken, 1637-1711; † verse alt. by Michael Kuhn
Tune: OLD HUNDREDTH, LM; Louis Bourgeois, c.1510-1561

## 147 All Grownups, All Children

Refrain

All grown-ups, all chil-dren, all moth-ers, all fa-thers are sis-ters and broth-ers in the fam-'ly of God.

Verses

1. I am a per-son. God made me spe-cial.
2. So man-y chil-dren, all of them dif-f'rent.
3. God has a fam-'ly with man-y peo-ple;

You are a per-son and you're spe-cial too.
God gave all peo-ple their own things to do.
Grown-ups and chil-dren who love God to-day.

We have our fam-'lies and friends we can play with.
All of God's chil-dren are sis-ters and broth-ers.
We get to-geth-er to care for each oth-er to

D.C.

There are so man-y good things we can do.
I know God loves me and God loves you too.
Wor-ship and learn how to fol-low God's way.

Text: Patricia Joyce Shelly, b.1951, © 1977
Tune: Patricia Joyce Shelly, b.1951, © 1977; acc. by Robert N. Roth, © 2000, GIA Publications, Inc.

## 148 Praise and Thanksgiving

Canon

1. Praise and thanks-giv-ing let ev-'ry-one bring
2. All peo-ple, join us and sing out God's praise.
3. May we go out from here God's love to share.

2.
Un - to our God for ev - 'ry good thing.
For ev - 'ry bless - ing your hap - py songs raise.
Sing - ing out God's love to all ev - 'ry - where.

3.
All to - geth - er joy - ful - ly sing!

Text: St. 1, Alsatian traditional; tr. Edith Lovell Thomas, alt.; st. 2-3, Marie Post, © 1987, CRC Publications, alt.
Tune: LOBET UND PREISET, 10 9 8; Alsatian traditional; acc. by Robert J. Batastini, b.1942, © 2000, GIA Publications, Inc.

## For the Beauty of the Earth     149

1. For the beau - ty of the earth, For the glo - ry
2. For the beau - ty of each hour Of the day and
3. For the joy of ear and eye, For the heart and
4. For the joy of hu - man love, Broth - er, sis - ter,
5. For your church, that ev - er - more Lifts its ho - ly
6. For your - self, best Gift Di - vine! To this world so

of the skies, For the love which from our birth
of the night, Hill and vale, and tree and flow'r,
mind's de - light, For the mys - tic har - mo - ny
par - ent, child, Friends on earth, and friends a - bove;
hands a - bove, Of - f'ring up on ev - 'ry shore
free - ly giv'n; Word In - car - nate, God's de - sign,

O - ver and a - round us lies:
Sun and moon, and stars of light:
Link - ing sense to sound and sight:     Lord of all, to
For all gen - tle thoughts and mild:
Its pure sac - ri - fice of love:
Peace on earth and joy in heav'n:

you we raise This our hymn of grate - ful praise.

Text: Folliot S. Pierpont, 1835-1917
Tune: DIX, 7 7 7 7 77; arr. from Conrad Kocher, 1786-1872, by William H. Monk, 1823-1889

## 150 Earth and All Stars

1. Earth and all stars, Loud rush-ing plan - ets
2. En - gines and steel, Loud pound-ing ham - mers
3. Class - rooms and labs, Loud boil - ing test tubes
4. Knowl edge and truth, Loud sound ing wis dom

Sing to the Lord a new song!

Hail, wind, and rain, Loud blow - ing snow - storm
Lime - stone and beams, Loud build - ing work - ers
Ath - lete and band, Loud cheer - ing peo - ple
Daugh - ter and son, Loud pray - ing mem - bers

Sing to the Lord a new song! God has done mar -

vel-ous things. I too sing prais - es with a new song!

Text: Herbert F. Brokering, b.1926
Tune: EARTH AND ALL STARS, 4 5 7 D with refrain; David N. Johnson
© 1968, Augsburg Fortress

## 151 'Tis the Gift to Be Simple

'Tis the gift to be sim-ple, 'tis the gift to be free, 'tis the

gift to come down where we ought to be, and when we find our-

selves in the place just right, 'twill be in the val - ley of

love and de-light. When true sim - plic - i - ty is gained to

bow and to bend we shan't be a-shamed, to turn, turn, will

be our de-light till by turn - ing, turn - ing we come round right.

Text: Shaker Song, 18th. C.
Tune: SIMPLE GIFTS; acc. Margaret W. Mealy, © 1984

## In the Bulb There Is a Flower   152

1. In the bulb there is a flow - er; In the
2. There's a song in ev - 'ry si - lence, Seek-ing
3. In our end is our be - gin - ning; In our

seed, an ap - ple tree; In co - coons, a hid - den
word and mel - o - dy; There's a dawn in ev - 'ry
time, in - fin - i - ty; In our doubt there is be -

prom - ise: But - ter - flies will soon be free! In the
dark - ness, Bring-ing hope to you and me. From the
liev - ing; In our life, e - ter - ni - ty. In our

cold and snow of win - ter There's a spring that waits to be,
past will come the fu - ture; What it holds, a mys - ter - y,
death, a res - ur - rec - tion; At the last, a vic - to - ry,

Un - re - vealed un-til its sea-son, Some-thing God a-lone can see.

Text: Natalie Sleeth, 1930-1992
Tune: PROMISE, 8 7 8 7 D; Natalie Sleeth, 1930-1992
© 1986, Hope Publishing Co.

## 153 Sing Out, Earth and Skies

Verses

Cantor:
All:

1. Come, O God of all the earth: Come to us, O
2. Come, O God of wind and flame: Fill the earth with
3. Come, O God of flash-ing light: Twin-kling star and
4. Come, O God of snow and rain: Show-er down up -
5. Come, O Jus - tice, Come, O Peace: Come and shape our

Cantor:

Right - eous One; Come, and bring our love to birth:
right - eous - ness; Teach us all to sing your name:
burn - ing sun; God of day and God of night:
on the earth; Come, O God of joy and pain:
hearts a - new; Come and make op - pres - sion cease:

All:

In the glo - ry of your Son.
May our lives your love con - fess.
In your light we all are one.
God of sor - row, God of mirth.
Bring us all to life in you.

Refrain

Sing out, earth and skies! Sing of the God who loves you!

Raise your joy-ful cries! Dance to the life a - round you!

Text: Marty Haugen, b.1950
Tune: SING OUT, 7 7 7 7 with refrain; Marty Haugen, b.1950
© 1985, GIA Publications, Inc.

## 154 Sing Our God Together

Refrain

Sing, O peo - ple, sing our God to - geth - er,

raise your voic - es: sing al - le - lu - ia!

**Verses**

1. Sing with one an - oth - er: Sing the love that gave us breath!
2. Dance the steps of beau - ty: Dance the love that gave us breath!
3. Serve all those who suf - fer: Serve the love that gave us breath!
4. Teach the way of Je - sus: Teach the love that gave us breath!
5. Seek the chil - dren's wis-dom: Seek the love that gave us breath!

Sing, each sis - ter, broth - er: Sing the God be - yond all death!
Dance, de - light and du - ty: Dance the God be - yond all death!
Serve, that love might con - quer: Serve the God be - yond all death!
Teach the way that frees us: Teach the God be - yond all death!
Seek God's way of free-dom: Seek the God be - yond all death!

Text: David Haas, b. 1957, and Marty Haugen, b. 1950
Tune: David Haas, b. 1957, and Marty Haugen, b. 1950
© 1993, GIA Publications, Inc.

## Praise to God 155

1. Praise to God, praise to God, For the green - ness
2. Thanks to God, thanks to God, For the gift of
3. Sing to God, sing to God, For the grace of

of the trees, For the beau - ty of the flow'rs, For the
friends in Christ, For the church, our house of faith, For the
Je - sus Christ, For the love of par - ent God, For the

blue-ness of the sky, For the great-ness of the sea.
gift of won - drous love, For the gift of end - less grace.
com-fort and the strength Of the Spir - it, ho - ly God.

Praise to God, praise to God, Now and for - ev - er-more.
Thanks to God, thanks to God, Now and for - ev - er-more.
Sing to God, sing to God, Now and for - ev - er-more.

Text: Nobuaki Hanaoka, © 1983, Japanese United Methodist Church
Tune: SAKURA, 6 7 7 7 7 6 6; Japanese traditional; tr. © 1983, Abingdon Press, harm. by Jonathan McNair, © 1993, Pilgrim Press

# 156 All Things Bright and Beautiful

**Refrain**

All things bright and beau - ti - ful, All
crea - tures great and small, All things wise and
won - der - ful, The Lord God made them all.

**Verses**

1. Each lit - tle flow'r that o - pens,    Each
2. The pur - ple - head - ed moun - tain,    The
3. The cold wind in the win - ter,    The
4. God gave us eyes to see them,    And

lit - tle bird that sings,    God made their glow - ing
riv - er run - ning by,    The sun - set, and the
pleas - ant sum - mer sun,    The ripe fruits in the
lips that we might tell    How great is God Al -

**D.C.**

col - ors, God made their ti - ny wings.
morn - ing That bright - ens up the sky.
gar - den, God made them ev - 'ry one.
might - y, Who has made all things well.

Text: Cecil F. Alexander, 1818-1895, alt.
Tune: ROYAL OAK, 7 6 7 6 with refrain; English Melody; adapted by Martin Shaw, 1875-1958

# All You Works of God  157

Text: Marty Haugen, b.1950
Tune: Marty Haugen, b.1950
© 1989, GIA Publications, Inc.

## 158 Holy God, We Praise Thy Name

1. Ho - ly God, we praise thy name! Lord of
2. Hark! the loud ce - les - tial hymn An - gel
3. Ho - ly Fa - ther, Ho - ly Son, Ho - ly

all, we bow be - fore thee; All on earth thy
choirs a - bove are rais - ing; Cher - u - bim and
Spir - it, Three we name thee, While in es - sence

scep - ter claim, All in heav'n a - bove a -
Ser - a - phim In un - ceas - ing cho - rus
on - ly One, Un - di - vid - ed God we

dore thee; In - fi - nite thy vast do - main,
prais - ing, Fill the heav'ns with sweet ac - cord:
claim thee, And a - dor - ing bend the knee,

*Repeat ad lib.*

Ev - er - last - ing is thy reign.
Ho - ly, ho - ly, ho - ly Lord!
While we own the mys - ter - y.

Text: *Grosser Gott, wir loben dich;* ascr. to Ignaz Franz, 1719-1790; tr. by Clarence Walworth, 1820-1900
Tune: GROSSER GOTT, 7 8 7 8 77; *Katholisches Gesangbuch,* Vienna, c.1774

## 159 Sing, Sing, Praise and Sing!

Refrain

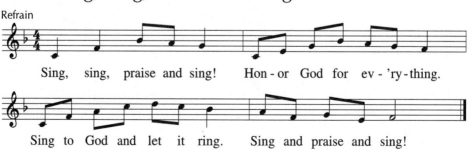

Sing, sing, praise and sing! Hon - or God for ev - 'ry-thing.

Sing to God and let it ring. Sing and praise and sing!

Verses

D.C.

1. Clap your hands, lift your voice, Praise our God and re - joice!
2. Full of joy, full of rest, Through our God, we are blessed.
3. Cym - bal, harp, vi - o - lin, Tam - bou - rine, all join in!

Text: Elizabeth Syré, South Africa, alt.
Tune: SING, SING, PRAISE AND SING, 66 with refrain; South African traditional; adapt. by Elizabeth Syré; acc. by Robert N. Roth, © 2000,
  GIA Publications, Inc.

## Sing Praise to Our Creator    160

1. Sing praise to our Cre - a - tor, Re -
2. To Je - sus Christ give glo - ry, God's
3. Now praise the Ho - ly Spir - it Poured

deemed of A - dam's race; God's chil - dren by a -
co - e - ter - nal Son; As mem - bers of his
forth up - on the earth, Who sanc - ti - fies and

dop - tion, Bap - tized in liv - ing grace.
bod - y We are in Christ made one.
guides us, Con - firmed in our re - birth.

O most ho - ly Trin - i - ty, Un - di - vid - ed u - ni - ty;

Ho - ly God, might - y God, God im - mor - tal, be a - dored!

Text: Omer Westendorf, 1916-1998; © 1962, World Library Publications, Inc.
Tune: GOTT VATER SEI GEPRIESEN, 76 76 with refrain; *Limburg Gesangbuch*, 1838; harm. by Healey Willan, 1880-1968, © 1958,
  Ralph Jusko Publications, Inc.

# 161 Praise to the Trinity

Refrain

In the night, in the day, we give praise to the Trin - i - ty, Cre -
a - tor, Re - deem - er, Sus - tain - er of life, sing - ing
praise, liv - ing praise, breath - ing praise to our God of glo - ry,
al - le - lu - ia for - ev - er, al - le - lu - ia!

Verses

1.-3. Blest are you, God of all Cre - a - tion, through your good - ness

we have life; bod - y, mind and voice, spir - it too, re - joice,
               hearts of thank-ful - ness, hands of play - ful - ness,
work of field and vine, now our bread and wine,

D.C.

voic - es re - sound - ing in praise.
sing - ing re - news all our days.
gift of the har - vest we bring.

Text: Rob Glover, b.1950
Tune: Rob Glover, b.1950
© 1994, Choristers Guild

# Good News 162

Verses

1. When Je - sus worked here on earth he
2. The eld - ers of the syn - a - gogue were
3. The way he lived was proof of it: he
4. So pass it on to - day, good friend: the

preached in his home - town, I - sa - iah's hopes
shocked by Mar - y's son, That he was des -
qui - et - ed our strife. The cross it - self he
mes - sage is the same. De - liv - 'rance Christ a -

now ful - filled, those claims of great re - nown.
tined to be the Christ for ev - 'ry - one.
would not flee e'en though it cost his life.
lone can give, for this to earth he came.

Refrain

To bring good news to the need - y, to make the

blind to see, the bro - ken hearts healed a - gain, to

1. set the cap - tive free.
2. cap - tive free.

Text: Howard S. Olson, © 1993
Tune: Almaz Belihu; Yemissrach Dimts Literature Program, Ethiopia, © 1993, Howard S. Olson; acc. by Rob Glover, © 2000, GIA Publications, Inc.

# 163 I Danced in the Morning

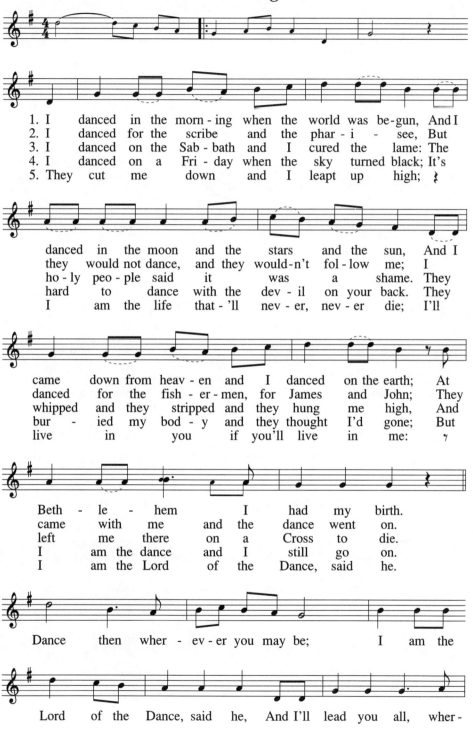

1. I danced in the morn-ing when the world was be-gun, And I
2. I danced for the scribe and the phar-i - see, But
3. I danced on the Sab-bath and I cured the lame: The
4. I danced on a Fri-day when the sky turned black; It's
5. They cut me down and I leapt up high;

danced in the moon and the stars and the sun, And I
they would not dance, and they would-n't fol-low me; I
ho-ly peo-ple said it was a shame. They
hard to dance with the dev-il on your back. They
I am the life that-'ll nev-er, nev-er die; I'll

came down from heav-en and I danced on the earth; At
danced for the fish-er-men, for James and John; They
whipped and they stripped and they hung me high, And
bur - ied my bod-y and they thought I'd gone; But
live in you if you'll live in me:

Beth - le - hem I had my birth.
came with me and the dance went on.
left me there on a Cross to die.
I am the dance and I still go on.
I am the Lord of the Dance, said he.

Dance then wher - ev-er you may be; I am the

Lord of the Dance, said he, And I'll lead you all, wher-

ev - er you may be, And I'll lead you all in the Dance, said he.

Text: Sydney Carter, b.1915, © 1963, Stainer & Bell, Ltd., London, England. (admin. by Hope Publishing Co.)
Tune: LORD OF THE DANCE, Irregular; adapted from a traditional Shaker melody by Sydney Carter, b.1915, © 1963, Stainer & Bell, Ltd., London, England. (admin. by Hope Publishing Co.)

## Praise to You, O Christ, Our Savior 164

Refrain

Praise to you, O Christ, our Sav-ior, Word of the Fa-ther, call-ing us to life;

Son of God who leads us to free-dom: glo-ry to you, Lord Je-sus Christ!

Verses

1. You are the Word who calls us out of dark - ness;
2. You are the one whom proph - ets hoped and longed for;
3. You are the Word who calls us to be ser - vants;
4. You are the Word who binds us and u - nites us;

you are the Word who leads us in - to light;
you are the one who speaks to us to - day;
you are the Word whose on - ly law is love;
you are the Word who calls us to be one;

you are the Word who brings us through the des - ert:
you are the one who leads us to our fu - ture:
you are the Word - made - flesh who lives a - mong us:
you are the Word who teach - es us for - give - ness:

D.C.

glo - ry to you, Lord Je - sus Christ!

Text: Bernadette Farrell, b.1957
Tune: Bernadette Farrell, b.1957
© 1986, Bernadette Farrell. Published by OCP Publications.

# 165 When Jesus Saw the Fishermen

Canon

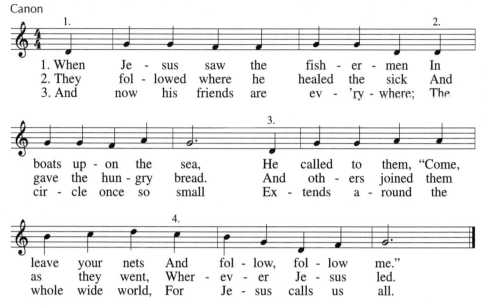

1. When Je - sus saw the fish - er - men In
2. They fol - lowed where he healed the sick And
3. And now his friends are ev - 'ry - where; The

boats up - on the sea, He called to them, "Come,
gave the hun - gry bread. And oth - ers joined them
cir - cle once so small Ex - tends a - round the

leave your nets And fol - low, fol - low me."
as they went, Wher - ev - er Je - sus led.
whole wide world, For Je - sus calls us all.

Text: Edith Agnew, © 1953, Westminster/John Knox Press
Tune: ST. STEPHEN, 8 6 8 6; Richard L. Van Oss, b.1953, © 1994, CRC Publications

# 166 The Lord, the Lord, the Lord Is My Shepherd

Refrain: The Lord, the Lord, the Lord is my shep-herd, The
1. You bring me rest in green, green pas - tures, You
2. My fear is gone for you are with me, Your

Lord, the Lord, the Lord is my shep-herd, The
lead me to the still, still wa - ters, You
rod and staff bring com - fort sure; Your

Lord, the Lord, the Lord is my shep - herd, The
guide me a - long your own right way, The
good - ness and mer - cy shall fol - low me, The

Lord is my shep-herd and I shall not want.

Text: African-American spiritual
Tune: THE LORD IS MY SHEPHERD, Irregular; African-American spiritual; harm. by Austin C. Lovelace, b.1919, © 1986, GIA Publications, Inc.

## Jesus Christ, Yesterday, Today and for Ever    167

Ostinato Refrain

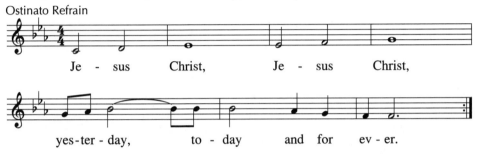

Je - sus Christ, Je - sus Christ,

yes-ter - day, to - day and for ev - er.

Text: Suzanne Toolan, SM, b.1927
Tune: Suzanne Toolan, SM, b.1927
© 1988, GIA Publications, Inc.

## Jesus in the Morning    168

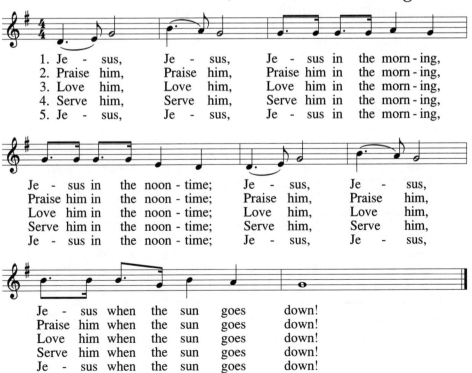

1. Je - sus, Je - sus, Je - sus in the morn-ing,
2. Praise him, Praise him, Praise him in the morn-ing,
3. Love him, Love him, Love him in the morn-ing,
4. Serve him, Serve him, Serve him in the morn-ing,
5. Je - sus, Je - sus, Je - sus in the morn-ing,

Je - sus in the noon - time; Je - sus, Je - sus,
Praise him in the noon - time; Praise him, Praise him,
Love him in the noon - time; Love him, Love him,
Serve him in the noon - time; Serve him, Serve him,
Je - sus in the noon - time; Je - sus, Je - sus,

Je - sus when the sun goes down!
Praise him when the sun goes down!
Love him when the sun goes down!
Serve him when the sun goes down!
Je - sus when the sun goes down!

Text: African-American folk song
Tune: African-American folk song

## 169 In Christ There Is No East or West

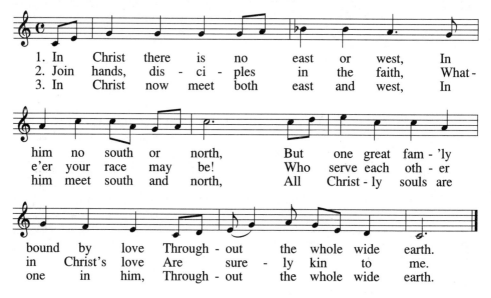

1. In Christ there is no east or west, In
2. Join hands, dis - ci - ples in the faith, What-
3. In Christ now meet both east and west, In

him no south or north, But one great fam - 'ly
e'er your race may be! Who serve each oth - er
him meet south and north, All Christ - ly souls are

bound by love Through - out the whole wide earth.
in Christ's love Are sure - ly kin to me.
one in him, Through - out the whole wide earth.

Text: Galatians 3:23; John Oxenham, 1852-1941
Tune: MC KEE, CM; African-American; adapt. by Harry T. Burleigh, 1866-1949

## 170 Jesus' Hands Were Kind Hands

1. Je - sus' hands were kind hands, do - ing good to all,
2. Take my hands, Lord Je - sus, let them work for you;

Heal - ing pain and sick - ness, bless - ing chil - dren small.
Make them strong and gen - tle, kind in all I do.

Wash - ing tir - ed feet, and sav - ing those who fall;
Let me watch you, Je - sus, till I'm gen - tle too,

Je - sus' hands were kind hands, do - ing good to all.
Till my hands are kind hands, quick to work for you.

Text: Margaret Cropper, 1886-1980, © 1979, Stainer & Bell, Ltd. (admin. by Hope Publishing Co.)
Tune: AU CLAIR DE LA LUNE, 11 11 D; Old French melody; harm. by Carlton R. Young, b.1926, © 1989, The United Methodist
   Publishing House

# Send Us Your Spirit 171

**Refrain**

*1.                                    2.

Come Lord Je-sus, send us your Spir-it, re-
new the face of the earth. Come Lord
Je-sus, send us your Spir-it, re-new the face of the
earth.

**Verses**

1. Come to us, Spir-it of God, breathe in us
2. Fill us with the fire of your love, burn in us
3. Send us the wings of new birth, fill all the

now, we sing to-geth-er. Spir-it of
now, bring us to-geth-er. Come to us,
earth with the love you have taught us. Let all cre-

hope and of light, fill our lives,
dwell in us, change our lives, O Lord,
a - tion now be shak-en with love,

**D.C.**

come to us, Spir-it of God.
come to us, Spir-it of God.
come to us, Spir-it of God.

*May be sung in canon.*

Text: David Haas, b.1957
Tune: David Haas, b.1957; acc. by Jeanne Cotter, b.1964
© 1981, 1982, 1987, GIA Publications, Inc.

# 172 Envía Tu Espíritu

Text: *Send out your spirit and renew the face of the earth;* Psalm 104:30; the Sequence of Pentecost; Bob Hurd, b.1950
Tune: Bob Hurd, b.1950; acc. by Craig Kingsbury, b.1952, © 1988, Bob Hurd
Published by OCP Publications.

## Veni Sancte Spiritus (Come, Holy Spirit)  173

Refrain

Ve - ni      San - cte  Spi - ri - tus;

Ve - ni      San - cte  Spi - ri - tus;

Ve - ni,     ve - ni   San - cte  Spi - ri - tus;

Ve - ni     San - cte      Spi - ri - tus.

Text: Pentecost Sequence; Christopher Walker, b.1947
Tune: Christopher Walker, b.1947
© 1981, 1982, Christopher Walker. Published by OCP Publications.

## O Breathe on Me, O Breath of God  174

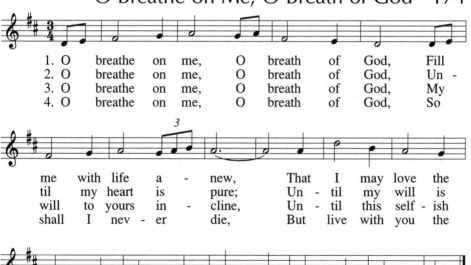

1. O   breathe  on  me,  O   breath  of  God,  Fill
2. O   breathe  on  me,  O   breath  of  God,  Un -
3. O   breathe  on  me,  O   breath  of  God,  My
4. O   breathe  on  me,  O   breath  of  God,  So

me   with  life   a  -  new,   That  I   may  love  the
til   my  heart  is   pure;   Un - til  my  will  is
will  to  yours  in  - cline,  Un - til  this  self - ish
shall  I   nev - er  die,   But  live  with  you  the

things  you  love,  And  do   what  you  would  do.
one   with  yours,  To   do   and  to   en - dure.
part  of   me   Glows  with  your  fire  di - vine.
per - fect  life  Of   your  e - ter - ni - ty.

Text: Edwin Hatch, 1835-1889
Tune: ST. COLUMBA, CM; Gaelic; harm. by A. Gregory Murray, OSB, 1905-1992, © Downside Abbey

# 175 O Holy Spirit, by Whose Breath

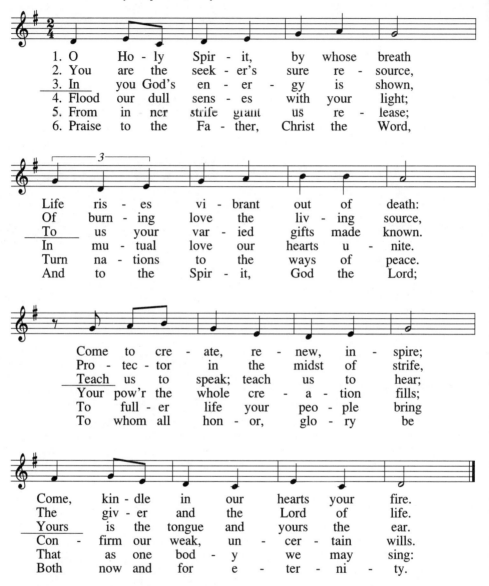

1. O Ho - ly Spir - it, by whose breath
2. You are the seek - er's sure re - source,
3. In you God's en - er - gy is shown,
4. Flood our dull sens - es with your light;
5. From in ner strife grant us re - lease;
6. Praise to the Fa - ther, Christ the Word,

Life ris - es vi - brant out of death:
Of burn - ing love the liv - ing source,
To us your var - ied gifts made known.
In mu - tual love our hearts u - nite.
Turn na - tions to the ways of peace.
And to the Spir - it, God the Lord;

Come to cre - ate, re - new, in - spire;
Pro - tec - tor in the midst of strife,
Teach us to speak; teach us to hear;
Your pow'r the whole cre - a - tion fills;
To full - er life your peo - ple bring
To whom all hon - or, glo - ry be

Come, kin - dle in our hearts your fire.
The giv - er and the Lord of life.
Yours is the tongue and yours the ear.
Con - firm our weak, un - cer - tain wills.
That as one bod - y we may sing:
Both now and for e - ter - ni - ty.

Text: *Veni, Creator Spiritus;* attr. to Rabanus Maurus, 776-865; tr. by John W. Grant, b.1919, © 1971
Tune: VENI CREATOR SPIRITUS, LM; Mode VIII; setting by Richard J. Wojcik, b.1923, © 1975, GIA Publications, Inc.

# Send Down the Fire 176

Text: Marty Haugen, b.1950
Tune: Marty Haugen, b.1950
© 1989, GIA Publications, Inc.

# 177 Spirit-Friend

1. God sends us his Spir - it     to be-friend and help us.
2. Dark - ened roads are clear - er,     heav - y bur - dens light - er,
3. Now we are God's peo - ple,     bond - ed by God's pres - ence,

Re - cre - ate and guide us,     Spir - it - Friend.
When we're walk - ing with our     Spir - it - Friend.
A - gents of God's pur - pose,     Spir - it - Friend.

Spir - it who en - liv - ens,     sanc - ti - fies, en - light - ens,
Now we need not fear the     pow - ers of the dark - ness.
Lead us for-ward ev - er,     slip - ping back-ward nev - er,

Sets us free, is now our     Spir - it - Friend.
None can o - ver - come our     Spir - it - Friend.
To your re - made world, our     Spir - it - Friend.

*Sing a., b., and c. after each stanza.*     Hand claps

a. Spir - it of our Mak - er,     Spir - it - Friend.
b. Spir - it of our Je - su,     Spir - it - Friend.
c. Spir - it of God's peo - ple,     Spir - it - Friend.

Text: Tom Colvin, b.1925
Tune: NATOMAH, 12 9 12 9 with refrain; Gonja folk song; adapt. by Tom Colvin, b.1925; acc. by Marty Haugen, b. 1950
© 1969, 1987, Hope Publishing Co.

# Isaiah 49    178

Text: Carey Landry
Tune: Carey Landry; arr. by Therese Edell
© 1975, Carey Landry and NALR. Published by OCP Publications.

# 179 Walking By Faith

Refrain

We are walk-ing by faith, we are walk-ing by faith, we are

walk - ing by faith to the king - dom! In

prayer we will lis - ten, in your wis - dom we will grow; we will

walk by faith till we come to the prom-ised land!

Verses

1. You are our God, and we your peo - ple; called by cre-
2. Je - sus the Lord, we will share in your love; walk-ing by
3. Ris - en from death, we are made new in you; walk-ing with

a - tion and the Spir - it. We hear your Word, and we will
faith, we will praise you. Heal-ing and for - giv - ing, we will
you, we tell your sto - ry. Filled with your Spir - it, we will

D.C.

live in you, and sing and praise you on the way!
join in your song, and sing and praise you on the way!
one day see your face, and sing and praise you on the way!

Text: David Haas, b.1957
Tune: David Haas, b.1957
© 1997, GIA Publications, Inc.

# Pues Si Vivimos / If We Are Living   180

```
1. Pues   si   vi - vi - mos      pa - ra  Él    vi - vi - mos,
1. If     we   are  liv - ing     we are  in    the   Lord,
2. En     es - ta   vi - da,      fru - tos  he - mos de  dar;
2. Through-out  our  lives        we have  fruit  to    bear.
3. En     la   tris - te - za     y  en   el    do - lor,
3. When   there  is   sad - ness,  when   there  is    pain
4. En     es - te   mun - do,     he - mos de en - con - trar
4. And    in   this  world        we will  al -  ways  find
```

```
y     si   mo - ri - mos     pa - ra  Él    mo - ri - mos.
and   if   we   die          we are  in    the   Lord,
las   o - bras  bue - nas     son  pa - ra of - ren - dar.
All   of   our  good works    are for   us    to    share.
en    la   be - lle - za      y  en   el    a -  mor
in    Christ the  Lord,       we have  love  to    gain.
gen - te   que  llo - ra      y  sin  con - so - lar.
those who  are  weep - ing,   sick in  heart and   mind.
```

```
Sea  que  vi - va - mos         o    que  mu - ra - mos,
for  if   we   live             or   if   we   die
Ya   sea  que  de - mos         o  que  re - ci - ba - mos,
Whe - ther  we   give,          or   we   re - ceive
Sea  que  su - fra - mos        o    que  go - ce - mos,
Whe - ther  we   suf - fer      or   we   re - joice,
Sea  que a - yu - de - mos      o  que al - i - men - te - mos,
They need  our   help,          they  need  our   care.
```

```
so - mos del  Señ - or,      so - mos del  Señ - or.
we be - long  to God,        we be - long  to God.
```

Text: Verse 1, Romans 14:8; traditional Spanish; translation by Deborah L. Schmitz, b.1969. © 1994, GIA Publications, Inc.
Tune: Traditional Spanish; arr. by Diana Kodner, b.1957. © 1994, GIA Publications, Inc.

# 181 Moved by the Gospel, Let Us Move

1. Moved by the Gos - pel, let us move With ev - 'ry gift and art. The im - age of cre - a - tive love In - dwells each hu - man heart. The Mak - er calls cre - a - tion good, So let us now ex - press With sound and col - or, stone and wood, The shape of ho - li - ness.

2. Let weav - ers form from bro - ken strands A tap - es - try of prayer. Let art - ists paint with skill - ful hands Their joy, la - ment, and care. Then mime the sto - ry: Christ has come. With flute and or - gan, rev - 'rence dance the word. With flute and or - gan, God's praise be ev - er heard.

3. O Spir - it, breathe a - mong us here; In - spire the work we do. May hands and voic - es, eye and ear At - test to life made new. In wor - ship and in dai - ly strife Cre - ate a - mong us still. Great Art - ist, form our com - mon life Ac - cord - ing to your will.

*God's chil - dren speak in dif - f'rent tongues, With dif - f'rent things to say, And dif - f'rent tasks and dif - f'rent toys, And man - y dif - f'rent ways, And some are dark, and some are fair, And all have dif - f'rent names, And all are fam - i - ly to me, And God loves us the same.

*Alternate text

Text: Ruth Duck, b.1947, © 1992, GIA Publications, Inc.; alt. text, Nancy Byrd Turner, 1880-1971, alt., © 1924, Sydney A. Weston
Tune: KINGSFOLD, CMD; English; harm. by Ralph Vaughan Williams, 1872-1958

# We Are Many Parts 182

Refrain

We are man-y parts, we are all one bod-y,
and the gifts we have we are giv-en to share.
May the Spir-it of love make us one in-deed;
one, the love that we share, one, our hope in de-
spair, one, the cross that we bear.

Verses

1. God of all, we look to you, we would be your
2. So my pain is pain for you, in your joy is
3. All you seek-ers, great and small, seek the great-est

D.C.

ser-vants true, let us be your love to all the world.
my joy, too; all is brought to-geth-er in the Lord.
gift of all; if you love, then you will know the Lord.

Text: 1 Corinthians 12, 13; Marty Haugen, b.1950
Tune: Marty Haugen, b.1950
© 1980, 1986, GIA Publications, Inc.

# 183 Gather Us In

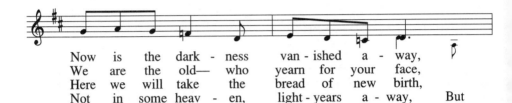

1. Here  in  this  place  new  light  is  stream - ing,
2. We  are  the  young—  our  lives  are  a  mys - t'ry,
3. Here  we  will  take  the  wine  and  the  wa - ter,
4. Not  in  the  dark  of  build ings  con - fin - ing,

Now  is  the  dark - ness  van - ished  a - way,
We  are  the  old—  who  yearn  for  your  face,
Here  we  will  take  the  bread  of  new  birth,
Not  in  some  heav - en,  light - years  a - way,  But

See  in  this  space  our  fears  and  our  dream - ings,
We  have  been  sung  through - out  all  of  his - t'ry,
Here  you  shall  call  your  sons  and  your  daugh - ters,
here  in  this  place  the  new  light  is  shin - ing,

Brought here  to  you  in  the  light  of  this  day.
Called  to  be  light  to  the  whole  hu - man  race.
Call  us  a - new  to  be  salt  for  the  earth.
Now  is  the  King - dom,  now  is  the  day.

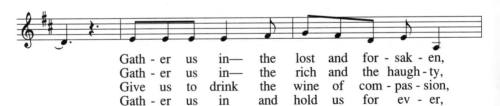

Gath - er  us  in—  the  lost  and  for - sak - en,
Gath - er  us  in—  the  rich  and  the  haugh - ty,
Give  us  to  drink  the  wine  of  com - pas - sion,
Gath - er  us  in  and  hold  us  for  ev - er,

Gath - er  us  in—  the  blind  and  the  lame;
Gath - er  us  in—  the  proud  and  the  strong;
Give  us  to  eat  the  bread  that  is  you;
Gath - er  us  in  and  make  us  your  own;

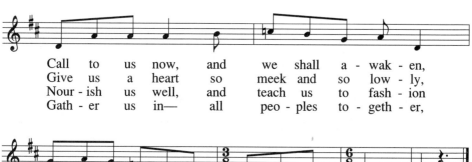

Call to us now, and we shall a - wak - en,
Give us a heart so meek and so low - ly,
Nour - ish us well, and teach us to fash - ion
Gath - er us in— all peo - ples to - geth - er,

We shall a - rise at the sound of our name.
Give us the cour-age to en - ter the song.
Lives that are ho - ly and hearts that are true.
Fire of love in our flesh and our bone.

Text: Marty Haugen, b.1950
Tune: GATHER US IN, Irregular; Marty Haugen, b.1950
© 1982, GIA Publications, Inc.

## I Come with Joy    184

1. I come with joy, a child of God, For -
2. I come with Chris - tians far and near To
3. As Christ breaks bread, and bids us share, Each
4. The Spir - it of the ris - en Christ, Un -
5. To - geth - er met, to - geth - er bound By

giv - en, loved, and free, The life of Je - sus
find, as all are fed, The new com - mu - ni -
proud di - vi - sion ends. The love that made us,
seen, but ev - er near, Is in such friend - ship
all that God has done, We'll go with joy, to

to re - call, In love laid down for me.
ty of love In Christ's com - mu - nion bread.
makes us one, And stran - gers now are friends.
bet - ter known, A - live a - mong us here.
give the world The love that makes us one.

Text: Brian Wren, b.1936, © 1971, 1995, Hope Publishing Co.
Tune: LAND OF REST, CM; American; harm. by Annabel M. Buchanan, 1888-1983, © 1938, 1966, J. Fisher and Bro.

# 185 All Are Welcome

1. Let us build a house where love can dwell And
2. Let us build a house where proph - ets speak, And
3. Let us build a house where love is found In
4. Let us build a house where hands will reach Be -
5. Let us build a house where all are named, Their

all can safe - ly live, A place where saints and
words are strong and true, Where all God's chil - dren
wa - ter, wine and wheat: A ban - quet hall on
yond the wood and stone To heal and strength-en,
songs and vi - sions heard And loved and treas - ured,

chil - dren tell How hearts learn to for -
dare to seek To dream God's reign a -
ho - ly ground, Where peace and jus - tice
serve and teach, And live the Word they've
taught and claimed As words with - in the

give. Built of hopes and dreams and vi - sions,
new. Here the cross shall stand as wit - ness
meet. Here the love of God, through Je - sus,
known. Here the out - cast and the stran - ger
Word. Built of tears and cries and laugh - ter,

Rock of faith and vault of grace; Here the
And as sym - bol of God's grace; Here as
Is re - vealed in time and space; As we
Bear the im - age of God's face; Let us
Prayers of faith and songs of grace, Let this

love of Christ shall end di - vi - sions:
one we claim the faith of Je - sus:
share in Christ the feast that frees us: All are wel - come,
bring an end to fear and dan - ger:
house pro-claim from floor to raft - er:

all are wel-come, all are wel-come in this place.

Text: Marty Haugen, b. 1950
Tune: TWO OAKS, 9 6 8 6 8 7 10 with refrain; Marty Haugen, b. 1950
© 1994, GIA Publications, Inc.

## We Are the Church 186

**Refrain**

I am the church! You are the church! We are the

church to - geth - er! All who fol - low Je - sus,

all a - round the world! Yes, we're the church to - geth-er!

**Verses**

1. The church is not a build - ing, the
2. We're man - y kinds of peo - ple, with
3. And when the peo - ple gath - er, there's

church is not a stee - ple, the church is not a
man - y kinds of fac - es, all col - ors and all
sing - ing and there's pray - ing, there's laugh - ing and there's

D.C.

rest - ing place, the church is a peo - ple.
a - ges, too, from all times and plac - es.
cry - ing some - times, all of it say - ing:

Text: Richard K. Avery and Donald S. Marsh
Tune: PORT JERVIS, 7 7 8 7 with refrain; Richard K. Avery and Donald S. Marsh
© 1972, Hope Publishing Co.

# 187 Stand Up, Friends

**Verses**

1. Praise the God who chang - es plac - es,
2. Praise the Rab - bi, speak - ing, do - ing
3. Praise the Breath of Love, whose free - dom
4. Praise, un - til we join the sing - ing

Leaves the loft - y seat, Wel - comes us with
All that God in - tends, Dy - ing, ris - ing,
Spreads our wak - ing wings, Lift - ing ev - 'ry
Far be - yond our sight, With the End - ing

warm em - bra - ces, Stoops to wash our feet.
faith re - new - ing, Call - ing us his friends.
blight and bur - den Till the spir - it sings;
and Be - gin - ning Danc - ing in the light.

**Refrain**

Stand up, friends! Hold your heads high! Free-dom is our

**1.**
song! Al - le - lu - ia! Free-dom is our song! Al - le - lu - ia!

**2.**
ia!

**D.C.** **Final ending**

Text: Brian Wren, b.1936, © 1986, Hope Publishing Co.
Tune: David Haas, b.1957, © 1993, GIA Publications, Inc.

# Two By Two   188

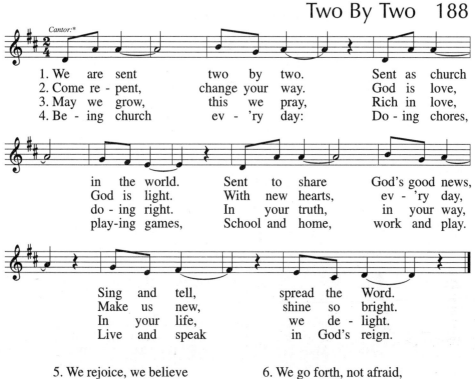

*Cantor:*

1. We are sent    two by two.    Sent as church
2. Come re - pent,    change your way.    God is love,
3. May we grow,    this we pray,    Rich in love,
4. Be - ing church    ev - 'ry day:    Do - ing chores,

in the world.    Sent to share    God's good news,
God is light.    With new hearts,    ev - 'ry day,
do - ing right.    In your truth,    in your way,
play-ing games,    School and home,    work and play.

Sing and tell,    spread the Word.
Make us new,    shine so bright.
In your life,    we de - light.
Live and speak    in God's reign.

5. We rejoice, we believe
Listen well, pray and sing.
We give thanks, we receive,
Share our gifts, love we bring.

6. We go forth, not afraid,
Care and serve old and new.
To the world, all you made,
With our God, two by two.

*This song may be sung as a Call and Response at the interval of one measure.*

Text: Rob Glover, b.1950
Tune: TWO BY TWO, 6 6 6 6; Rob Glover, b.1950
© 2000, GIA Publications, Inc.

# There Is One Lord   189

**Ostinato Refrain**

There is one Lord, one faith, one bap - tis-m,

There is one God who is Fa - ther of all.

Text: Ephesians 4; Taizé Community, 1984
Tune: Jacques Berthier, 1923-1994
© 1984, Les Presses de Taizé, GIA Publications, Inc., agent

# 190  As a Fire Is Meant for Burning

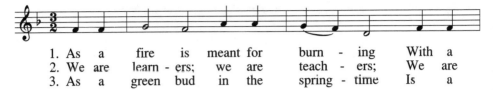

1. As a fire is meant for burn - ing With a
2. We are learn - ers; we are teach - ers; We are
3. As a green bud in the spring - time Is a

bright and warm-ing flame, So the church is meant for
pil - grims on the way. We are seek - ers; we are
sign of life re - newed, So may we be signs of

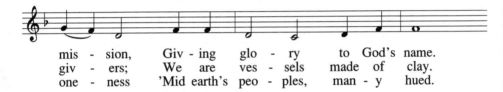

mis - sion, Giv - ing glo - ry to God's name.
giv - ers; We are ves - sels made of clay.
one - ness 'Mid earth's peo - ples, man - y hued.

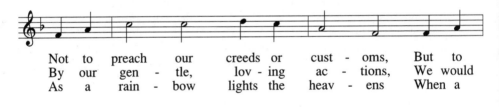

Not to preach our creeds or cust - oms, But to
By our gen - tle, lov - ing ac - tions, We would
As a rain - bow lights the heav - ens When a

build a bridge of care, We join hands a - cross the
show that Christ is light. In a hum - ble, lis-t'ning
storm is past and gone, May our lives re - flect the

na - tions, Find - ing neigh - bors ev - 'ry - where.
Spir - it, We would live to God's de - light.
ra - diance Of God's new and glor-ious dawn.

Text: Ruth Duck, b.1947, © 1992, GIA Publications, Inc.
Tune: BEACH SPRING, 8 7 8 7 D; The Sacred Harp, 1844; harm. by Marty Haugen, b.1950, © 1985, GIA Publications, Inc.

# Now Thank We All Our God     191

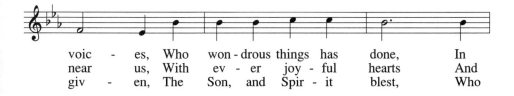

1. Now thank we all our God      With      hearts and hands and
2. O      may this gra-cious God      Through all   our  life  be
3. All    praise and thanks to God     The      Fa - ther now  be

voic  -  es,   Who   won - drous things has     done,      In
near     us,  With   ev  -  er   joy - ful    hearts     And
giv   -  en,  The    Son,  and  Spir - it    blest,     Who

whom his world re  -  joic   -  es;  Who,  from  our  moth-ers'
bless - ed  peace to      cheer      us;  Pre  -  serve  us    in   his
reigns  in  high - est     heav   -   en,   E   -  ter - nal,  Tri - une

arms,      Hath    blest   us    on    our   way     With
grace,     And     guide   us    in    dis - tress,    And
God,       Whom    earth  and  heav'n  a  -  dore;    For

count-less gifts  of    love,    And   still   is    ours   to  -  day.
free    us  from  all    sin,    Till   heav - en   we    pos - sess.
thus    it  was,  is     now,    And   shall  be    ev  -  er - more.

Text: *Nun danket alle Gott;*  Martin Rinkart, 1586-1649; tr. by Catherine Winkworth, 1827-1878, alt.
Tune: NUN DANKET, 6 7 6 7 6 6 6 6; Johann Crüger, 1598-1662; harm. by A. Gregory Murray, OSB, 1905-1992

# 192 Bring Forth the Kingdom

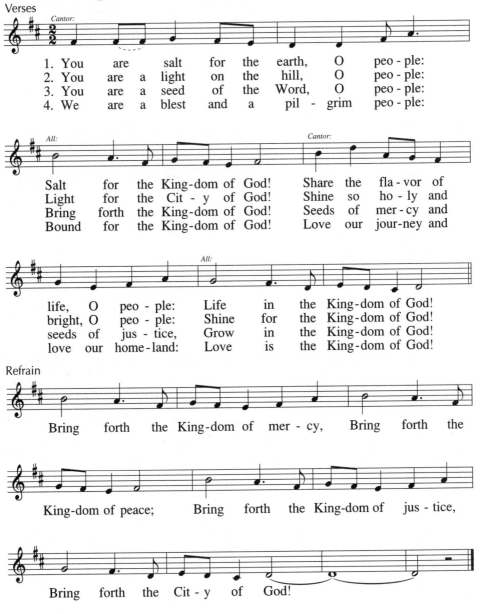

Verses

Cantor:

1. You    are    salt    for    the    earth,    O    peo - ple:
2. You    are    a    light    on    the    hill,    O    peo - ple:
3. You    are    a    seed    of    the    Word,    O    peo - ple:
4. We    are    a    blest    and    a    pil - grim    peo - ple:

All:                                              Cantor:

Salt    for    the    King-dom of God!    Share    the    fla - vor    of
Light    for    the    Cit - y    of God!    Shine    so    ho - ly    and
Bring    forth    the    King-dom of God!    Seeds    of    mer - cy    and
Bound    for    the    King-dom of God!    Love    our    jour-ney    and

All:

life,    O    peo - ple:    Life    in    the    King-dom of God!
bright, O    peo - ple:    Shine    for    the    King-dom of God!
seeds    of    jus - tice,    Grow    in    the    King-dom of God!
love    our    home-land:    Love    is    the    King-dom of God!

Refrain

Bring    forth    the    King-dom of    mer - cy,    Bring    forth    the

King-dom of peace;    Bring    forth    the    King-dom of    jus - tice,

Bring    forth    the    Cit - y    of    God!

Text: Marty Haugen, b.1950
Tune: Marty Haugen, b.1950
© 1986, GIA Publications, Inc.

# We Are Marching   193

*Alternate text: dancing, singing, praying...*

Text: South African
Tune: South African
© 1984, Utryck, Walton Music Corporation, agent

# 194 On Eagle's Wings

**Verse 1**

1. You who dwell in the shel-ter of the Lord, who a-bide in his shad-ow for life, say to the Lord: "My ref-uge, my rock in whom I trust!"

**Refrain**

And he will raise you up on ea-gle's wings, bear you on the breath of dawn, make you to shine like the sun, and

*Last time to coda* ⊕ *To verses*

hold you in the palm of his hand. 2. The

**Verse 2**

snare of the fowl-er will nev-er cap-ture you, and fam-ine will bring you no fear: un-der his wings your

**D.S.**

ref-uge, his faith-ful-ness your shield.

**Verse 3**

3. You need not fear the ter-ror of the night, nor the ar-row that flies by day; though thou-sands fall a-bout you, near you it shall not come.

**D.S.**

**Verse 4**

4. For to his an-gels he's giv-en a com-mand to guard you in all of your ways; up-on their hands they will bear you up, lest you dash your foot a-gainst a stone.

**D.S.**

**✛ Coda**

And hold you, hold you in the palm of his hand.

Text: Psalm 91; Michael Joncas, b.1951
Tune: Michael Joncas, b.1951

# 195 Halleluya! We Sing Your Praises

Refrain

Hal - le - lu - ya! We sing your prais-es, all our

*Claps:*

hearts are filled with glad - ness. Hal - le - lu - ya! We sing your

prais-es, all our hearts are filled with glad - ness.

Verses

1. Christ the Lord to us said: I am
2. Now he sends us all out, strong in

wine, I am bread, I am wine, I am
faith, free of doubt, strong in faith, free of

bread, give to all who thirst and hun - ger.
doubt, to pro - claim the joy - ful Gos - pel.

Text: South African
Tune: South African
© 1984, Utryck, Walton Music Corporation, agent

# 196 We Shall Overcome

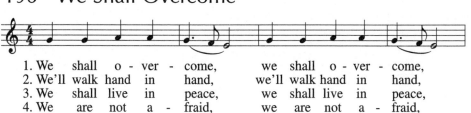

1. We shall o - ver - come, we shall o - ver - come,
2. We'll walk hand in hand, we'll walk hand in hand,
3. We shall live in peace, we shall live in peace,
4. We are not a - fraid, we are not a - fraid,

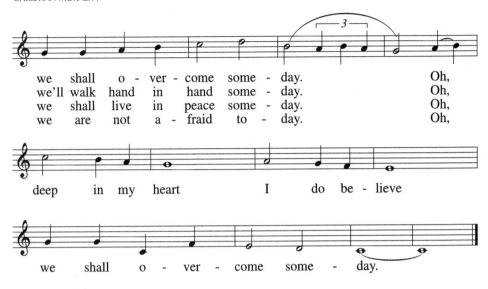

|3|

we shall o - ver - come some - day. Oh,
we'll walk hand in hand some - day. Oh,
we shall live in peace some - day. Oh,
we are not a - fraid to - day. Oh,

deep in my heart I do be - lieve

we shall o - ver - come some - day.

5. We shall stand together...
6. The truth will make us free...
7. The Lord will see us through...
8. We shall be like him...
9. The whole wide world around...

Text: adapt. by Zilphia Horton, Frank Hamilton, Guy Carawan, and Pete Seeger, © 1960, 1963, Ludlow Music
Tune: adapt. by Zilphia Horton, Frank Hamilton, Guy Carawan, and Pete Seeger, © 1960, 1963, Ludlow Music;
     harm. by J. Jefferson Cleveland, b.1937, from *Songs of Zion*, harm. © 1981, by Abingdon Press

## You Are My Shepherd 197

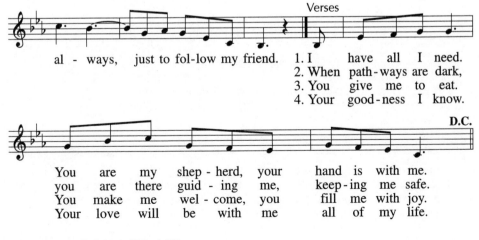

Refrain

You are my shep-herd, you are my friend. I want to fol-low you

al - ways, just to fol-low my friend.

Verses

1. I have all I need.
2. When path-ways are dark,
3. You give me to eat.
4. Your good-ness I know.

D.C.

You are my shep - herd, your hand is with me.
you are there guid - ing me, keep-ing me safe.
You make me wel - come, you fill me with joy.
Your love will be with me all of my life.

Text: Based on Psalm 23; Christopher Walker, b.1947
Tune: Christopher Walker, b.1947
© 1985, Christopher Walker. Published by OCP Publications.

## 198 Take, O Take Me As I Am

Take, O take me as I am; sum - mon out what I shall
be; set your seal up - on my heart and live in me.

Text: John L. Bell, b.1949
Tune: John L. Bell, b.1949
© 1994, Iona Community, GIA Publications, Inc., agent

## 199 Jesu, Jesu

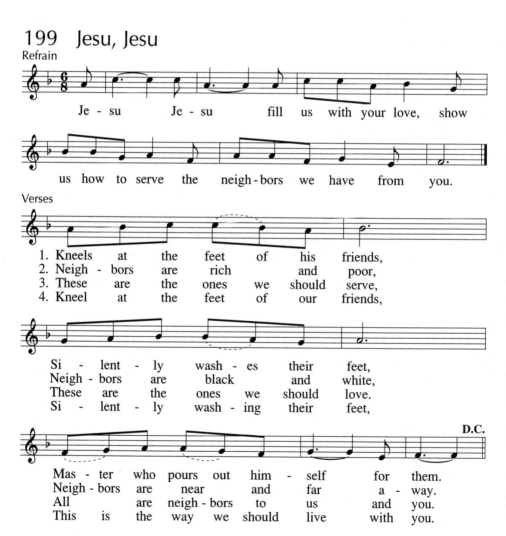

Refrain

Je - su Je - su fill us with your love, show
us how to serve the neigh - bors we have from you.

Verses

1. Kneels at the feet of his friends,
2. Neigh - bors are rich and poor,
3. These are the ones we should serve,
4. Kneel at the feet of our friends,

Si - lent - ly wash - es their feet,
Neigh - bors are black and white,
These are the ones we should love.
Si - lent - ly wash - ing their feet,

D.C.

Mas - ter who pours out him - self for them.
Neigh - bors are near and far a - way.
All are neigh - bors to us and you.
This is the way we should live with you.

Text: Tom Colvin, b.1925
Tune: CHEREPONI, Irregular; Ghana folk song; adapt. Tom Colvin, b.1925; acc. by Jane M. Marshall, b.1924
© 1969, and arr. © 1982, Hope Publishing Co.

# The Servant Song    200

1., 6. Will you let me be your ser - vant, Let me be as
2. We are pil - grims on a jour - ney, We are trav - 'lers
3. I will hold the Christ-light for you In the night-time
4. I will weep when you are weep - ing; When you laugh I'll
5. When we sing to God in heav - en We shall find such

Christ to you; Pray that I may have the grace to
on the road; We are here to help each oth - er
of your fear; I will hold my hand out to you,
laugh with you. I will share your joy and sor - row
har - mo - ny, Born of all we've known to - geth - er

Let you be my ser - vant, too.
Walk the mile and bear the load.
Speak the peace you long to hear.
'Til we've seen this jour - ney through.
Of Christ's love and ag - o - ny.

Text: Richard Gillard
Tune: Richard Gillard; harm. by Betty Pulkingham, b.1929
© 1977, Scripture in Song

# Ubi Caritas / Live in Charity    201

**Refrain**

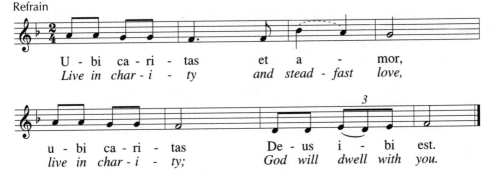

U - bi ca - ri - tas et a - mor,
*Live in char - i - ty* *and stead - fast love,*

u - bi ca - ri - tas De - us i - bi est.
*live in char - i - ty;* *God will dwell with you.*

Text: 1 Corinthians 13:2-8; *Where charity and love are found, God is there;* Taizé Community, 1978
Tune: Jacques Berthier, 1923-1994
© 1979, Les Presses de Taizé, GIA Publications, Inc., agent

## 202 Be Not Afraid

Verse 1

1. You shall cross the bar-ren des - ert, but you shall not die of thirst. You shall wan-der far in safe-ty though you do not know the way. You shall speak your words in for-eign lands and all will un - der - stand. You shall see the face of God and live.

Refrain

Be not a - fraid. I go be - fore you al - ways. Come, fol-low me, and I will give you rest.

Verse 2

2. If you pass through rag - ing wa-ters in the sea, you shall not drown. If you walk a-mid the burn-ing flames, you shall not be harmed. If you stand be - fore the

pow'r of hell and death is at your side,

know that I am with you through it all. **D.S.**

Verse 3

3. Bless-ed are your poor, for the king-dom shall be

theirs. Blest are you that weep and mourn, for

one day you shall laugh. And if wick-ed tongues in-

sult and hate you all be-cause of me,

**D.S.**

bless-ed, bless-ed are you!

Text: Isaiah 43:2-3, Luke 6:20ff; Bob Dufford, SJ, b.1943
Tune: Bob Dufford, SJ, b.1943; acc. by Sr. Theophane Hytrek, OSF, 1915-1992
© 1975, 1978, Robert J. Dufford, SJ, and New Dawn Music. Published by OCP Publications.

# 203  City of God

Verses 1, 2

1. A-wake from your slum-ber! A - rise from your
2. We are sons of the morn-ing; we are daugh-ters of

sleep! A new day is dawn - ing
day. The One who has loved us

for all those who weep. The peo - ple in
has bright-ened our way. The Lord of all

dark - ness have seen a great light. The Lord of our
kind - ness has called us to be a light for his

long - ing has con-quered the night.
peo - ple to set their hearts free.

Refrain %

Let us build the cit-y of God. May our tears be

turned in - to danc - ing! For the Lord, our light and our

love, has turned the night in - to day!

Verse 3

3. God is light; in him there is no dark-ness. Let us walk in his light, his chil - dren, one and all. O com-fort my peo - ple; make gen-tle your words. Pro - claim to my cit-y the day of her birth.

Verse 4

4. O cit-y of glad-ness, now lift up your voice. Pro - claim the good tid - ings that all may re - joice!

Text: Dan Schutte, b.1947
Tune: Dan Schutte, b.1947; acc. by Robert J. Batastini, b. 1942

## 204 God Has Chosen Me

**Verses**

1. God has cho - sen me, God has cho - sen me to
2. God has cho - sen me, God has cho - sen me to
3. God is call - ing me, God is call - ing me in

bring good news to the poor. God has cho - sen me,
set a - light a new fire. God has cho - sen me,
all whose cry is un - heard. God is call - ing me,

God has cho - sen me to bring new sight to those
God has cho - sen me to bring to birth a new
God is call - ing me to raise up the voice with no

search - ing for light: God has cho - sen me, cho - sen me:
king - dom on earth: God has cho - sen me, cho - sen me:
pow - er or choice: God is call - ing me, call - ing me:

**Refrain**

And to tell the world that God's king - dom is near, to re -

move op - pres - sion and break down fear, yes, God's

1. time is near, God's time is near, God's
2. time is near.

Text: Bernadette Farrell, b.1957
Tune: Bernadette Farrell, b.1957
© 1990, Bernadette Farrell. Published by OCP Publications.

# We Are Called 205

1. Come! Live in the light! Shine with the
2. Come! O - pen your heart! Show your
3. Sing! Sing a new song! Sing of that

joy and the love of the Lord! We are called
mer - cy to all those in fear! We are called
great day when all will be one! God will reign,

to be light for the king - dom, to
to be hope for the hope - less so all
and we'll walk with each oth - er as

live in the free - dom of the cit - y of God!
ha - tred and blind - ness will be no more!
sis - ters and broth - ers u - nit - ed in love!

We are called to act with jus-tice, we are called to

love ten - der - ly, we are called to serve one an - oth-er;

to walk hum - bly with God!

Text: Micah 6:8; David Haas, b.1957
Tune: David Haas, b.1957

## 206 Guide My Feet

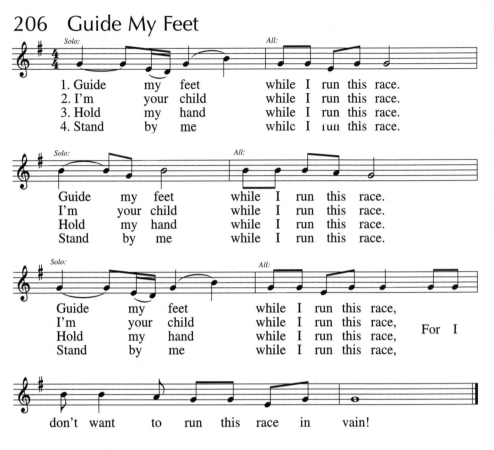

1. Guide my feet while I run this race.
2. I'm your child while I run this race.
3. Hold my hand while I run this race.
4. Stand by me while I run this race.

Guide my feet while I run this race.
I'm your child while I run this race.
Hold my hand while I run this race.
Stand by me while I run this race.

Guide my feet while I run this race,
I'm your child while I run this race,
Hold my hand while I run this race, For I
Stand by me while I run this race,

don't want to run this race in vain!

Text: African-American traditional
Tune: African-American traditional; acc. by Robert J. Batastini, b.1942, © 2000, GIA Publications, Inc.

## 207 This Is My Commandment

Canon

This is my com-mand-ment, that you love one an-oth-er that your

joy may be full. This is my com-mand-ment, that you

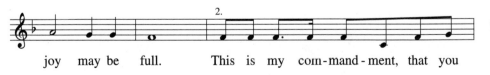

love one an-oth-er that your joy may be full, that your

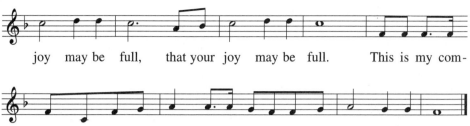

joy may be full, that your joy may be full. This is my com-

mand-ment, that you love one an-oth-er that your joy may be full.

Text: John 15:11-12
Tune: Traditional

## This Little Light of Mine  208

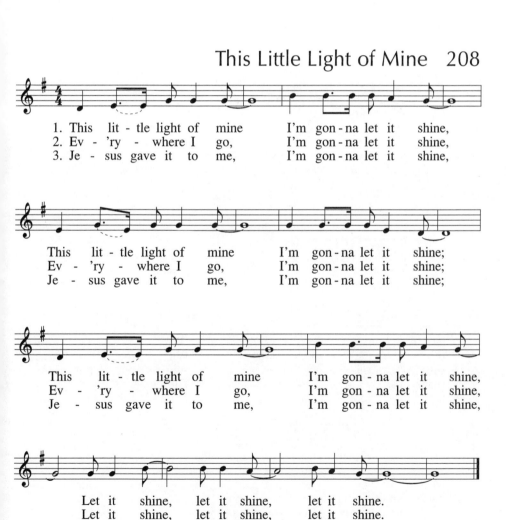

1. This lit - tle light of mine   I'm gon-na let it shine,
2. Ev - 'ry - where I go,   I'm gon-na let it shine,
3. Je - sus gave it to me,   I'm gon-na let it shine,

This lit - tle light of mine   I'm gon-na let it shine;
Ev - 'ry - where I go,   I'm gon-na let it shine;
Je - sus gave it to me,   I'm gon-na let it shine;

This lit - tle light of mine   I'm gon-na let it shine,
Ev - 'ry - where I go,   I'm gon-na let it shine,
Je - sus gave it to me,   I'm gon-na let it shine,

Let it shine, let it shine, let it shine.
Let it shine, let it shine, let it shine.
Let it shine, let it shine, let it shine.

Text: African-American spiritual
Tune: African-American spiritual; harm. by Horace Clarence Boyer, © 1992

## 209 The Summons

1. Will you come and fol - low me If I but
2. Will you leave your - self be - hind If I but
3. Will you let the blind - ed see If I but
4. Will you love the 'you' you hide If I but
5. Lord, your sum - mons ech - oes true When you but

call your name? Will you go where
call your name? Will you care for
call your name? Will you set the
call your name? Will you quell the
call my name. Let me turn and

you don't know And nev - er be the same?
cruel and kind And nev - er be the same?
pris - 'ners free And nev - er be the same?
fear in - side And nev - er be the same?
fol - low you And nev - er be the same.

Will you let my love be shown, Will you
Will you risk the hos - tile stare Should your
Will you kiss the lep - er clean, And do
Will you use the faith you've found To re -
In your com - pa - ny I'll go Where your

let my name be known, Will you let my
life at - tract or scare? Will you let me
such as this un - seen, And ad - mit to
shape the world a - round, Through my sight and
love and foot - steps show. Thus I'll move and

life be grown In you and you in me?
an - swer prayer In you and you in me?
what I mean In you and you in me?
touch and sound In you and you in me?
live and grow In you and you in me.

Text: John L. Bell, b.1949, © 1987, Iona Community, GIA Publications, Inc., agent
Tune: KELVINGROVE, 7 6 7 6 777 6; Scottish traditional; arr. by John L. Bell, b.1949, © 1987, Iona Community, GIA Publications, Inc., agent

# Lord, You Give the Great Commission    210

1. Lord, you give the great com - mis - sion: "Heal the sick and
2. Lord, you call us to your serv - ice: "In my name bap -
3. Lord, you make the com - mon ho - ly: "This my bod - y,
4. Lord, you show us love's true meas - ure: "Fa - ther, what they
5. Lord, you bless with words as - sur - ing: "I am with you

preach the word." Lest the Church ne - glect its mis - sion,
tize and teach." That the world may trust your prom - ise,
this my blood." Let us all, for earth's true glo - ry,
do, for - give." Yet we hoard as pri - vate treas - ure
to the end." Faith and hope and love re - stor - ing,

And the Gos - pel go un - heard, Help us wit - ness
Life a - bun - dant meant for each, Give us all new
Dai - ly lift life heav - en - ward, Ask - ing that the
All that you so free - ly give. May your care and
May we serve as you in - tend, And, a - mid the

to your pur - pose With re - newed in - teg - ri - ty;
fer - vor, draw us Clos - er in com - mun - i - ty;
world a - round us Share your chil - dren's lib - er - ty;
mer - cy lead us To a just so - ci - e - ty;
cares that claim us, Hold in mind e - ter - ni - ty;

With the Spir - it's gifts em - pow'r us For the work of min - is - try.

Text: Jeffery Rowthorn, b.1934, © 1978, Hope Publishing Co.
Tune: HYMN TO JOY, 8 7 8 7 D; arr. from Ludwig van Beethoven, 1770-1827, by Edward Hodges, 1796-1867

# 211   Here I Am, Lord

Verses

1. I, the Lord of sea and sky, I have heard my
2. I, the Lord of snow and rain, I have borne my
3. I, the Lord of wind and flame, I will tend the

peo - ple cry.   All who dwell in dark and sin
peo - ple's pain.   I have wept for love of them.
poor and lame.   I will set a feast for them.

My hand will save.   I who made the
They turn a - way.   I will break their
My hand will save.   Fin - est bread I

stars of night,   I will make their dark - ness bright.
hearts of stone,   Give them hearts for love a - lone.
will pro - vide   Till their hearts be sat - is - fied.

Who will bear my light to them?   Whom shall I send?
I will speak my word to them.   Whom shall I send?
I will give my life to them.   Whom shall I send?

Refrain

Here I am, Lord.   Is it I, Lord?   I have heard you

call - ing in the night.   I will go, Lord, if you

lead me.   I will hold your peo - ple in my heart.

Text: Isaiah 6; Dan Schutte, b.1947
Tune: Dan Schutte, b.1947; arr. by Michael Pope, SJ, and John Weissrock
© 1981, Daniel L. Schutte and New Dawn Music. Published by OCP Publications.

# You Are Mine 212

**Verses**

1. I will come to you in the si - lence,
2. I am hope for all who are hope - less,
3. I am strength for all the des - pair - ing,
4. am the Word that leads all to free - dom, I

1. I will lift you from all your fear.
2. I am eyes for all who long to see. In the
3. heal - ing for the ones who dwell in shame.
4. am the peace the world can - not give.

1. You will hear my voice, I claim you as my choice, be
2. shad - ows of the night, I will be your light,
3. All the blind will see, the lame will all run free, and
4. I will call your name, em - brac - ing all your pain, stand

1. still and know I am here. *(To verse 2)*
2. come and rest in me. *(To refrain)*
3. all will know my name. *(To refrain)*
4. up, now walk, and live! *(To refrain)*

**Refrain**

Do not be a - fraid, I am with you. I have called you

each by name. Come and fol - low me, I will bring you

D.C.

home; I love you and you are mine.

4. I

Text: David Haas, b.1957
Tune: David Haas, b.1957
© 1991, GIA Publications, Inc.

## 213 Love One Another

Refrain

Cantor:*

Love one an-oth-er.  
Care for each oth-er.

Love one an-oth-er,  
Care for each oth-er,

as I have loved you.  
as I care for you.

Verses

1. Turn the oth-er cheek and give to those who do you
2. Love your en-e-mies and pray for those who bring you

wrong. Walk a mile or two for them.  
down. We are chil-dren of the earth,

D.C.

Share what-ev-er you have.  
one great fam-'ly of God.

*For the refrain, the assembly echoes the cantor at the space of one measure.*

Text: Matthew 5:38-48; Rob Glover, b.1950
Tune: Rob Glover, b.1950
© 2000, GIA Publications, Inc.

## 214 Blest Are They

Verses 1-3

1. Blest are they, the poor in spir - it,
2. Blest are they, the low - ly ones,
3. Blest are they who show mer - cy,

theirs is the king - dom of God.  
they shall in - her - it the earth.  
mer - cy shall be theirs.

Text: Matthew 5:3-12; David Haas, b.1957
Tune: David Haas, b.1957
© 1985, GIA Publications, Inc.

## 215 Circle Round for Freedom

**Refrain**

Cir - cle round for free-dom, cir - cle round for peace, for all of us im - pris-oned, cir-cle for re - lease. Cir-cle for the plan-et, cir - cle for each soul. For the chil-dren of our chil - dren, keep the cir - cle whole.

**Verses**

1. Free-dom for foe and fam-i - ly, Free - dom for ev - 'ry race and creed, Free-dom for all hu - man - i - ty: May all hearts be free. (May all hearts be free.)
2. Peace in our homes and cit - ies, Peace with all lands and na - tions, Peace with our friends and en - e - mies: May we all know peace. (May we all know peace.)
3. Cir - cle our lives with free - dom, Cir - cle our world with bless-ed peace, Cir - cle each bod - y, mind and soul: Make our u - ni-verse whole. (Make our u - ni-verse whole.)

*Optional echo:*

**D.C.**

Text: Refrain text, Linda Hirschhorn, © 1982, Tara Publications; verse text, Rob Glover, b.1950, © 1997, GIA Publications, Inc.
Tune: Refrain music, Linda Hirschhorn, © 1982, Tara Publications; verse music and arr., Rob Glover, b.1950, © 1997, GIA Publications, Inc.

# Dona Nobis Pacem  216

Canon

Do - na    no - bis    pa  -  cem,  pa - cem.

Do - na no - bis pa  -  cem.

Do  -  na    no  -  bis  pa - cem.

Do - na    no - bis  pa  -  cem.

Do  -  na    no  -  bis  pa - cem.

Do - na    no - bis  pa  -  cem.

Text: *Grant us peace;* Unknown
Tune: Traditional; acc. by Diana Kodner, b.1957, © 1994, GIA Publications, Inc.

## 217 A Means of Your Peace

1. Make me, Lord, a means of your peace;
2. Mas - ter, grant that I may not seek so

make me, O Lord, a means of your love. In this
much con - so - la - tion as to con - sole, Un - der -

world, de - spair-ing and sad, make me a
stand-ing as to un - der - stand, so much to be

source of cour-age and joy. Where there is ha - tred,
loved as rath-er to love. Help me to see in

let me bring love, where there is harm, your par - don to
giv-ing to all how we in turn re - ceive from your

soothe. Help me bring faith where there is but
hand, How we are par - doned as we for -

doubt, and where it is dark, the light of your truth.
give, and how we, in death, are born to new life.

Text: Based on the *Prayer of St. Francis of Assisi,* adapt. by Timothy Valentine, SJ
Tune: Timothy Valentine, SJ; arr. by Timothy Valentine, SJ and Peter Valentine
© 1999, GIA Publications, Inc.

## 218 I Say "Yes," Lord / Digo "Sí," Señor

Verses

*(Invocation)*

I say "Yes," my Lord. I say
Di - go "Sí," Se - ñor. Di - go

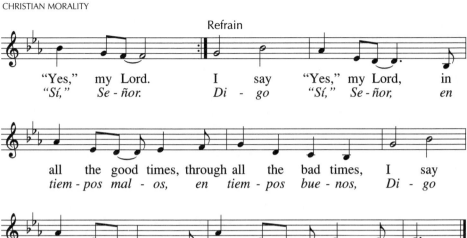

Refrain

"Yes," my Lord. I say "Yes," my Lord, in
"Sí," Se - ñor. Di - go "Sí," Se - ñor, en

all the good times, through all the bad times, I say
tiem - pos mal - os, en tiem - pos bue - nos, Di - go

"Yes," my Lord to ev - 'ry word you speak.
"Sí," Se - ñor a to - do lo que ha - blas.

Text: Donna Peña, b.1955
Tune: Donna Peña, b.1955; arr. by Marty Haugen, b.1950
© 1989, GIA Publications, Inc.

## Lord of All Nations, Grant Me Grace  219

*1. 2. 3.

1. Lord of all na - tions, grant me grace To
2. Break down the wall that would di - vide Your
3. For - give me, Lord, where I have erred By
4. Give me your cour - age, Lord, to speak When -
5. With your own love may I be filled And

4.

love all peo - ple, ev - 'ry race To see each mor - tal
chil - dren, Lord, on ev - 'ry side. My neigh-bor's good let
love - less act and thought-less word. Make me to see the
ev - er strong op - press the weak. Should I my - self as
by your Ho - ly Spir - it willed, That all whose lives are

as I ought, My kin - dred, whom your love has bought.
me pur - sue, Let Chris - tian love bind warm and true.
wrong I do Will cru - ci - fy my Lord a - new.
vic - tim live, Re - mem-b'ring you, may I for - give.
touched by mine, May know your heal - ing touch di - vine.

*May be sung as a two or four-voice canon.

Text: Philippians 2:1-18; Olive W. Spannaus, b.1916, © 1969, Concordia Publishing House
Tune: TALLIS' CANON, LM; Thomas Tallis, c.1505-1585

# 220 O God of Love, O King of Peace

1. O God of love, O King of peace, Make
2. Whom shall we trust but you, O Lord? Where
3. Where saints and an - gels dwell a - bove, All

wars through - out the world to cease; Our vio - lent ways help
rest but on your faith - ful word? None ev - er called on
hearts are joined in ho - ly love; O bind us in that

us con - tain; Give peace, O God, give peace a - gain!
you in vain; Give peace, O God, give peace a - gain!
heav'n - ly chain; Give peace, O God, give peace a - gain!

*May be sung as a two or four-voice canon.*

Text: Henry W. Baker, 1821-1877
Tune: TALLIS' CANON, LM; Thomas Tallis, c.1505-1585

# 221 Uyai Mose / Come All You People

*Harmony:*

U - ya - i mo - se, ti - na - ma - te Mwa - ri,
*Come all you peo - ple, come and praise your Mak - er,*

U - ya - i mo - se, ti - na - ma - te Mwa - ri,
*Come all you peo - ple, come and praise your Mak - er,*

U - ya - i mo - se, ti - na - ma - te Mwa - ri,
*Come all you peo - ple, come and praise your Mak - er,*

U - ya - i mo - se zvi - no.
*Come now and wor - ship the Lord.*

Text: Alexander Gondo
Tune: Alexander Gondo; arr. by John L. Bell, b.1949, © 1994, The Iona Community, GIA Publications, Inc., agent

## Baptized in Water 222

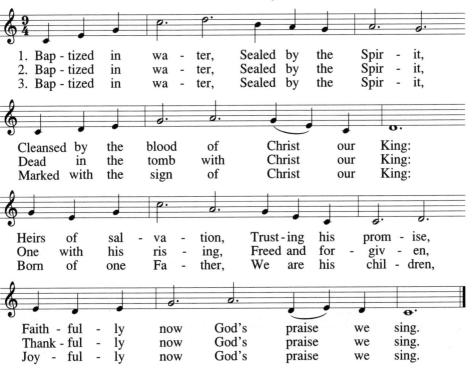

1. Bap - tized in wa - ter, Sealed by the Spir - it,
2. Bap - tized in wa - ter, Sealed by the Spir - it,
3. Bap - tized in wa - ter, Sealed by the Spir - it,

Cleansed by the blood of Christ our King:
Dead in the tomb with Christ our King:
Marked with the sign of Christ our King:

Heirs of sal - va - tion, Trust-ing his prom - ise,
One with his ris - ing, Freed and for - giv - en,
Born of one Fa - ther, We are his chil - dren,

Faith - ful - ly now God's praise we sing.
Thank - ful - ly now God's praise we sing.
Joy - ful - ly now God's praise we sing.

Text: Michael Saward, b.1932, © 1982, Jubilate Hymns, Ltd. (admin. by Hope Publishing Co.)
Tune: BUNESSAN, 5 5 8 D; Gaelic melody; acc. by Robert J. Batastini, b.1942, © 1999, GIA Publications, Inc.

## You Have Put on Christ 223

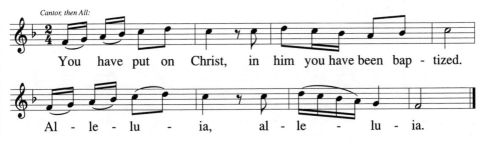

Cantor, then All:

You have put on Christ, in him you have been bap - tized.

Al - le - lu - ia, al - le - lu - ia.

Music: Howard Hughes, SM, © 1977, ICEL

## Christ Will Be Your Strength 224

Christ will be your strength! Learn to know and fol-low him!

Text: David Haas, b.1957
Tune: David Haas, b.1957
© 1988, GIA Publications, Inc.

## 225 With a Shepherd's Care

Refrain

With a shep-herd's care, God leads us. With a fa-ther's strength, God guides us. With a moth-er's love, God nur-tures us, and cra-dles us in gen-tle arms.

Verses

1. When we are lost, and can-not find the way, God
2. When we are weak, and cares press all a-round, God
3. When we are scared, and feel so all a-lone, God

cares for us and keeps us safe. For
strength-ens us to face each day. For
loves us and is by our side. For

God is our light and our faith-ful guide, and
God is our rock and our sav-ing help, and
God is our hope and our con-stant friend, and

D.C.

leads us with a shep-herd's care.
guides us with a fa-ther's strength.
nur-tures with a moth-er's love.

Text: James J. Chepponis, b.1956
Tune: James J. Chepponis, b.1956
© 1992, GIA Publications, Inc.

# Somebody's Knockin' at Your Door  226

Some-bod - y's knock-in' at your door; Some-bod - y's

knock-in' at your door; O sin - ner, why don't you

an - swer? Some-bod - y's knock-in' at your door.

*Solo:* *All:*

1. Knocks like Je - sus,
2. Can't you hear him?    Some-bod - y's knock-in' at your door.
3. Je - sus calls you,
4. Can't you trust him?

*Solo:* *All:*

Knocks like Je - sus,
Can't you hear him?    Some-bod - y's knock-in' at your door.
Je - sus calls you,
Can't you trust him?

O sin - ner, why don't you an - swer?

Some-bod - y's knock-in' at your door.

Text: African-American spiritual
Tune: SOMEBODY'S KNOCKIN', Irregular; African-American spiritual; harm. by Richard Proulx, b.1937, © 1986, GIA Publications, Inc.

## 227 Healer of Our Every Ill

Refrain

Heal - er of our ev - 'ry ill, light of each to - mor - row,

give us peace be - yond our fear, and hope be - yond our sor - row.

Verses

1. You who know our fears and sad - ness,
2. In the pain and joy be - hold - ing,
3. Give us strength to love each oth - er,
4. You who know each thought and feel - ing,

Grace us with your peace and glad - ness,
How your grace is still un - fold - ing,
Ev - 'ry sis - ter, ev - 'ry broth - er,
Teach us all your way of heal - ing,

D.C.

Spir - it of all com - fort: fill our hearts.
Give us all your vi - sion: God of love.
Spir - it of all kind - ness: be our guide.
Spir - it of com - pas - sion: fill each heart.

Text: Marty Haugen, b.1950
Tune: Marty Haugen, b.1950
© 1987, GIA Publications, Inc.

## 228 Standin' in the Need of Prayer

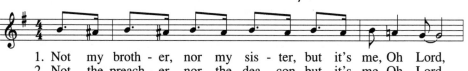

1. Not my broth - er, nor my sis - ter, but it's me, Oh Lord,
2. Not the preach - er, nor the dea - con, but it's me, Oh Lord,
3. Not my fa - ther, nor my moth - er, but it's me, Oh Lord,
4. Not the stran - ger, nor my neigh - bor, but it's me, Oh Lord,

Stand-in' in the need of prayer; Not my broth-er, nor my sis-ter,
Stand-in' in the need of prayer; Not the preach-er, nor the dea-con,
Stand-in' in the need of prayer; Not my fa-ther, nor my moth-er,
Stand-in' in the need of prayer; Not the stran-ger, nor my neigh-bor,

but it's me, Oh Lord, Stand-in' in the need of prayer.
but it's me, Oh Lord, Stand-in' in the need of prayer.
but it's me, Oh Lord, Stand-in' in the need of prayer. It's
but it's me, Oh Lord, Stand-in' in the need of prayer.

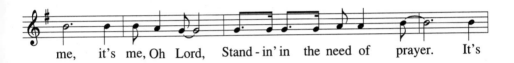

me, it's me, Oh Lord, Stand-in' in the need of prayer. It's

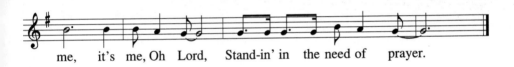

me, it's me, Oh Lord, Stand-in' in the need of prayer.

Text: African-American spiritual
Tune: African-American spiritual

# Nada Te Turbe / Nothing Can Trouble 229

Ostinato Refrain

Na-da te tur-be, na-da te_es-pan-te. Quien a Dios tie-ne
*Noth-ing can trou-ble, noth-ing can fright-en. Those who seek God shall*

na-da le fal-ta. So-lo Dios bas-ta.
*nev-er go want-ing. God a-lone fills us.*

Text: St. Teresa of Jesus; Taizé Community, 1986, 1991
Tune: Jacques Berthier, 1923-1994
© 1986, 1991, Les Presses de Taizé, GIA Publications, Inc., agent

## 230 Hold Us in Your Mercy: Penitential Litany

Hold us in your mer - cy. Hold us in your mer - cy.

Hold us in your mer - cy. Hold us in your mer - cy.

*(Invocation)* Hold us in your mer - cy.

*(Invocation)* Hold us in your mer - cy.

Hold us in your mer - cy. Hold us in your mer - cy.

Hold us in your mer - cy. Hold us in your mer - cy.

Hold us in your mer - cy. Hold us in your mer - cy.

Text: Rory Cooney, b.1952
Tune: Gary Daigle, b.1957
© 1993, GIA Publications, Inc.

## When Jesus the Healer 231

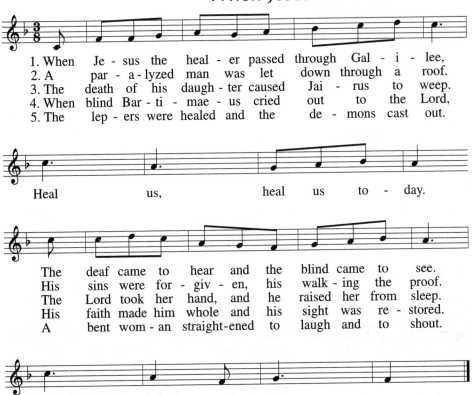

1. When Je - sus the heal - er passed through Gal - i - lee,
2. A par - a - lyzed man was let down through a roof.
3. The death of his daugh - ter caused Jai - rus to weep.
4. When blind Bar - ti - mae - us cried out to the Lord,
5. The lep - ers were healed and the de - mons cast out.

Heal us, heal us to - day.

The deaf came to hear and the blind came to see.
His sins were for - giv - en, his walk - ing the proof.
The Lord took her hand, and he raised her from sleep.
His faith made him whole and his sight was re - stored.
A bent wom - an straight-ened to laugh and to shout.

Heal us, Lord Je - sus.

Text: Peter D. Smith, b.1938
Tune: HEALER, 11 6 11 5; Peter D. Smith, b.1938; acc. by Robert N. Roth
© 1978, Stainer & Bell, Ltd. (admin. by Hope Publishing Co.)

## Eat This Bread 232

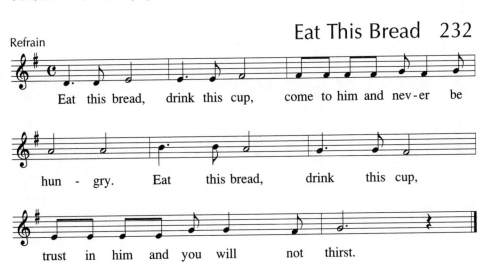

Refrain

Eat this bread, drink this cup, come to him and nev - er be

hun - gry. Eat this bread, drink this cup,

trust in him and you will not thirst.

Text: John 6; adapt. by Robert J. Batastini, b.1942, and the Taizé Community
Tune: Jacques Berthier, 1923-1994
© 1984, Les Presses de Taizé, GIA Publications, Inc., agent

## 233 Friends, All Gather 'Round

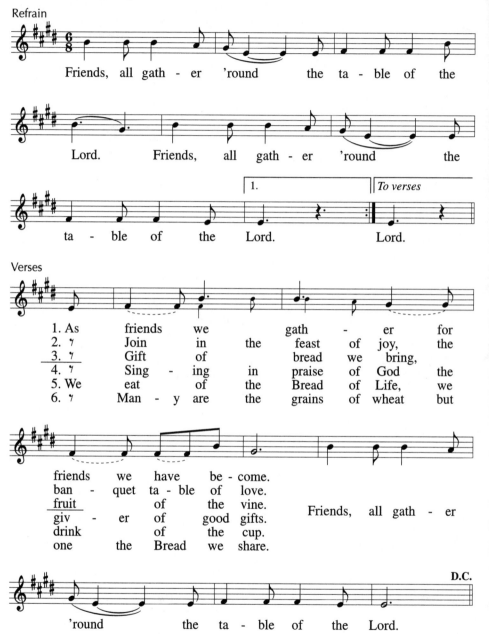

Refrain

Friends, all gath - er 'round the ta - ble of the
Lord. Friends, all gath - er 'round the
ta - ble of the Lord. Lord.

1. | To verses

Verses

1. As friends we gath - er for
2. ⁊ Join in the feast of joy, the
3. ⁊ Gift of bread we bring,
4. ⁊ Sing - ing in praise of God the
5. We eat of the Bread of Life, we
6. ⁊ Man - y are the grains of wheat but

friends we have be - come.
ban - quet ta - ble of love.
fruit of the vine.
giv - er of good gifts.
drink of the cup.
one the Bread we share.

Friends, all gath - er

D.C.

'round the ta - ble of the Lord.

Text: Joseph Doucet and Carey Landry
Tune: Joseph Doucet and Carey Landry; arr. by Paul Page
© 1979, NALR. Published by OCP Publications.

## All Who Hunger, Gather Gladly   234

1. All who hun - ger, gath - er glad - ly;
2. All who hun - ger, nev - er stran - gers,
3. All who hun - ger, sing to - geth - er;

Ho - ly man - na is our bread. Come from wil - der -
Seek - er, be a wel-come guest. Come from rest - less -
Je - sus Christ is liv - ing bread. Come from lone - li -

ness and wan - d'ring. Here, in truth, we will be fed.
ness and roam-ing. Here, in joy, we keep the feast.
ness and long - ing. Here, in peace, we have been led.

You that yearn for days of full - ness,
We that once were lost and scat - tered
Blest are those who from this ta - ble

All a - round us is our food. Taste and see the
In com - mun - ion's love have stood. Taste and see the
Live their days in grat - i - tude. Taste and see the

grace e - ter - nal. Taste and see that God is good.
grace e - ter - nal. Taste and see that God is good.
grace e - ter - nal. Taste and see that God is good.

Text: Sylvia G. Dunstan, 1955-1993, © 1991, GIA Publications, Inc.
Tune: HOLY MANNA, 8 7 8 7 D; William Moore, fl.1830; harm. by Charles Anders, b.1929, © 1969, *Comtemporary Worship I: Hymns*

## 235 I Am the Bread of Life / Yo Soy el Pan de Vida

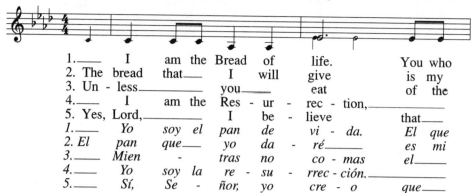

1. ___ I am the Bread of life. You who
2. The bread that___ I will give is my
3. Un - less___ you___ eat of the
4. ___ I am the Res - ur - rec - tion,___
5. Yes, Lord,___ I be - lieve that___

1. ___ Yo soy el pan de vi - da. El que
2. El pan que___ yo da - ré___ es mi
3. ___ Mien - tras no co - mas el___
4. ___ Yo soy la re - su - rrec - ción.___
5. ___ Sí, Se - ñor, yo cre - o que___

come to me shall not hun - ger;___ and who be -
flesh for the life of the world,___ and if you
flesh of the Son of Man___ and___
I___ am the life.___ If you be -
you___ are the Christ,___ the___

vie - ne_a mí no ten - drá ham - bre.___ El que
cuer - po___ vi - da del mun - do,___ y el que
cuer - po del hi - jo del hom - bre,___ y___
Yo___ soy la vi - da.___ El que
tú e - res el Cris - to,___ El___

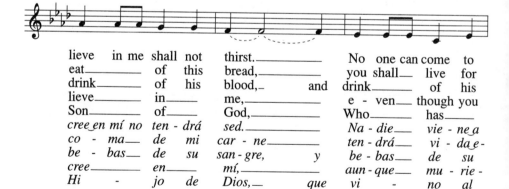

lieve in me shall not thirst.___ No one can come to
eat___ of this bread,___ you shall___ live for
drink___ of his blood,_ and drink___ of his
lieve___ in___ me,___ e - ven___ though you
Son___ of___ God,___ Who___ has___

cree_en mí no ten - drá sed.___ Na - die___ vie - ne_a
co - ma___ de mi car - ne___ ten - drá___ vi - da_e-
be - bas___ de su san - gre, y be - bas___ de su
cree___ en___ mí,___ aun - que___ mu - rie -
Hi - jo de Dios, _ que vi - no al

me          un - less   the____  Fa - ther    beck - ons.
ev - er,_____  you  shall____ live    for       ev - er.
blood,     you    shall  not have life  with - in   you.
die,_____   you  shall____ live   for       ev - er.
come     in - to_____  the_____   world.____
*mí*_____   *mien - tras el Pa - dre    lla - me.*
*ter - na,_____  ten - drá____ vi - da_e - ter - na.*
*san - gre,   no   ten - drá____ vi - da    en   ti.*
*ra,_____   ten - drá vi - da    e - ter - na.*
*mun - do_____  pa - ra    sal - var - nos.*

And   I   will   raise   you   up,        and   I   will
*Yo   le   re - su - ci - ta - ré,        Yo   le   re -*

raise        you   up,      and   I   will   raise        you
*su - ci - ta - ré,        Yo   le   re - su - ci - ta -*

up         on    the    last        day.
*ré         el    di - a        de_El.*

Text: John 6; Suzanne Toolan, SM, b.1927
Tune: BREAD OF LIFE, Irregular with refrain; Suzanne Toolan, SM, b.1927
© 1966, 1970, 1986, 1993, GIA Publications, Inc.

## 236  Pan de Vida

Refrain

\* *Pan de Vi - da,*      *cuer-po del Se - ñor,*

cup of bless - ing,      blood of Christ the Lord.

At this ta - ble      the last shall be first,      \*\* *po -*

*der es ser - vir,*      *por-que Dios es a - mor.*

Verses

1. { We are the dwell-ing of God,
\*\*\* 2. *Us - te - des me lla - man "Se - ñor,"*      *me in-*
3. { There is no Jew or Greek,

fra - gile and wound-ed and weak.      We are the
*cli - no a la - var - les los pies:*      *Ha - gan lo*
there is no slave or free:      there is no

bod - y of Christ,      called to be      the com -
*mis - mo, hu - mil - des, sir - vién - do - se*
wom-an or man;      on - ly heirs      of the

D.C.

pas - sion of God.
*u - nos a o - tros.*
prom - ise of God.

\* *Bread of Life, body of the Lord,*      \*\**power is for service, because God is Love.*
\*\*\**You call me "Lord," and I bow to wash your feet:*
*you must do the same, humbly serving each other.*

Text: John 13:1-15, Galatians 3:28-29; Bob Hurd, b.1950, and Pia Moriarty
Tune: Bob Hurd, b.1950; acc. by Craig Kingsbury, b.1952
© 1988, Bob Hurd and Pia Moriarty. Published by OCP Publications.

# We Come to Your Table   237

Verses

1. Gen - tle   Je - sus,   ris - en   Lord,
2. Bring - ing   gifts   of   all   we   are.
3. In   your   bod - y   we   find   life,
4. In   your   bod - y   we   are   one,
5. Je - sus   Sav - ior,   liv - ing   bread!
6. You   in - vite   us,   we   re - joice!

we come to your

ta - ble;

with   our   hearts   so   full   of   joy,
gifts   of   life   and   love   and   joy,
life   you   give   for   us   to   share.
one   with   you   and   one   an - oth - er.
Bread   of   heav - en,   bread   of   hope,
We   re - mem - ber,   we   give   thanks!

we come to your ta - ble.

Refrain

We come, we come,

we come to your ta - ble.

We come, we come,

we come to your ta - ble.

Text: Carey Landry
Tune: Carey Landry
© 1973, NALR. Published by OCP Publications.

# 238 Take and Eat

**Refrain**

Take and eat; take and eat: this is my bod - y giv-en up for you. Take and drink; take and drink: this is my blood giv - en up for you.

**Verses**

1. I am the Word that spoke and light was made;
2. I am the way that leads the ex - ile home;
3. I am the Lamb that takes a - way your sin;
4. I am the cor - ner - stone that God has laid;
5. I am the light that came in - to the world;
6. I am the first and last, the Liv - ing One;

I am the seed that died to be re - born;
I am the truth that sets the cap - tive free;
I am the gate that guards you night and day;
A cho - sen stone and pre - cious in his eyes;
I am the light that dark - ness can - not hide;
I am the Lord who died that you might live;

I am the bread that comes from heav'n a - bove;
I am the life that rais - es up the dead;
You are my flock: you know the shep-herd's voice;
You are God's dwell - ing place, on me you rest;
I am the morn - ing star that nev - er sets;
I am the bride-groom, this my wed - ding song;

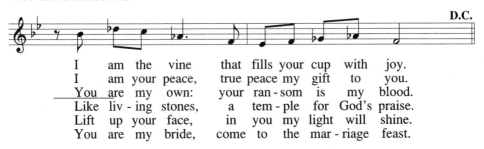

D.C.

I am the vine that fills your cup with joy.
I am your peace, true peace my gift to you.
You are my own: your ran-som is my blood.
Like liv-ing stones, a tem-ple for God's praise.
Lift up your face, in you my light will shine.
You are my bride, come to the mar-riage feast.

Text: Verse text, James Quinn, SJ, b.1919, © 1989. Used by permission of Selah Publishing Co., Inc., Kingston, NY 12401, North American agent.;
  refrain text, Michael Joncas, b.1951, © 1989, GIA Publications, Inc.
Tune: Michael Joncas, b.1951, © 1989, GIA Publications, Inc.

## I Received the Living God   239

**Refrain**

I re-ceived the liv-ing God, and my heart is full of
joy.     I re-ceived the liv-ing God, and my heart is full of joy.

**Verses**

1. Je - sus said: "I am the Bread Knead-ed
2. Je - sus said: "I am the Vine, And my
3. Je - sus said: "I am the Way, And my
4. Je - sus said: "I am the Truth; If you
5. Je - sus said: "I am the Life Far from

long to give you life; You who will par-take of
branch-es you shall be; Come and drink the sav-ing
Fa - ther longs for you; So I come to bring you
fol - low close to me, You will know me in your
whom no thing can grow, But re - ceive this liv-ing

D.C.

me Need not ev - er fear to die."
cup, Till the King - dom you shall see."
home To be one with him a - new."
heart, And my word shall make you free."
bread, And my Spir - it you shall know."

Text: Anonymous; verse 2, Alan J. Hommerding, b.1956, © 1994, World Library Publications, Inc.
Tune: LIVING GOD, 7 7 7 7 with refrain; Anonymous; harm. by Richard Proulx, b.1937, © 1986, GIA Publications, Inc.

# 240 Song of the Body of Christ / Canción del Cuerpo de Cristo

Refrain

We come to share our sto - ry, we
*Ve - ni-mos a de-cir del mis - te - rio,* y par -

come to break the bread, We come to know our
*tir el pan de vi - da. Ve - ni-mos a sa - ber de*

ris - ing from the dead.
*nues - tra e - ter - ni - dad.*

Verses

1. We come as your peo - ple, we
2. We are called to heal the bro - ken, to be
3. Bread of life and cup of prom - ise, in this
4. You will lead and we shall fol - low, you will
5. We will live and sing: "A - lo - ha," "Al - le -
   (live and sing your prais - es,)

come as your own, u - nit - ed with each
hope for the poor, we are called to feed the
meal we all are one. In our dy - ing and our
be the breath of life; liv - ing wa - ter, we are
lu - ia" is our song. May we live in love and

D.C.

oth - er, love finds a home.
hun - gry at our door.
ris - ing, may your king - dom come.
thirst - ing for your light.
peace our whole life long.

Verses

1. Ve - ni - mos, co - mo su pueb - lo en es -
2. Nos lla - ma pa - ra cu - rar y
3. Pan de vi - da y co - pa de pro - me - sa, so - mos
4. Nos guia - rás y te se - gui - re - mos, por - que
5. Vi - vi - re - mos can - tan - do "A - lo - ha." "A - le -

pí - ri - tu de ver - dad. U - ni - dos en su a -
ser su es - per - an - za. So - mos su - yos pa - ra_a - li - men -
u - no en es - ta co - mi - da. Ven - drá su rei - no_en
e - res la luz que bus - ca - mos. En el di - a o en la
lu - ya" es nues - tra can - ción. Por siem - pre vi - vi -

D.C.

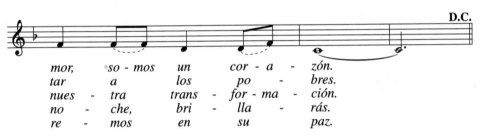

mor, so - mos un cor - a - zón.
tar a los po - bres.
nues - tra trans - for - ma - ción.
no - che, bri - lla - rás.
re - mos en su paz.

Text: David Haas, b.1957, Spanish translation by Donna Peña, b.1955
Tune: NO KE ANO' AHI AHI, Irregular, Hawaiian traditional, arr. by David Haas, b.1957
© 1989, GIA Publications, Inc.

# 241 Come and Eat This Living Bread

Refrain

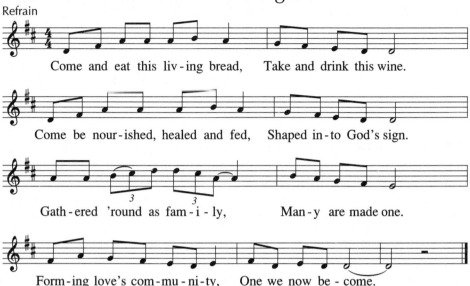

Come and eat this liv-ing bread, Take and drink this wine.

Come be nour-ished, healed and fed, Shaped in-to God's sign.

Gath-ered 'round as fam-i-ly, Man-y are made one.

Form-ing love's com-mu-ni-ty, One we now be-come.

Verses

1. Saint and sinner welcome in to this meal of harmony.
   Lonely people, next of kin journey toward the glory tree.
   Gathered strangers, scattered sheep, at this table all are fed.
   Blood and body bonds run deep as your kingdom feast is spread.

2. May we see the Christ revealed in the breaking of the bread.
   Living stories, holy meals, we become what we are fed.
   Broken, shattered, fragile life, now received by you and me.
   Eating, drinking, joy and strife, Gospel living sets us free.

3. See the Christ in saddened sighs, blood poured out in every land.
   Wounded people, wailing cries lie upon our outstretched hands.
   Jesus is the way through death; truth beyond the present rage.
   Life unfolding, healing breath now enfleshed in youth and age.

4. Bless us, Lord, and these your gifts, fruit of vine and human hands.
   With our hearts and minds we lift all the goodness of these lands.
   Praise and thanks we shout and sing, from your bounty we are blessed.
   Joyfully all gifts we bring to receive our Lord and guest.

5. Death and life in water meet, drenching us in floods of light.
   Marking us with oil so sweet, clothing us in glorious white.
   Priest and prophet, spirit led, we are God's new living sign.
   Feeding on this holy bread, drinking of this holy wine.

6. Witnessing to love and peace, hands of blessing we remain.
   Helping fear and hate to cease, we bring forth God's wondrous reign.
   Strength and power here we find, given in this kingdom feast.
   We go forth to heal and sign everyone, both great and least.

Text: Rob Glover, b.1950, © 1997, GIA Publications, Inc.
Tune: ADORO TE DEVOTE, 7 5 7 5 D; verses and arr. by Rob Glover, b.1950, © 1997, GIA Publications, Inc.

## One Bread, One Body  242

Text: 1 Corinthians 10:16; 17, 12:4, Galatians 3:28; the *Didache* 9; John Foley, SJ, b.1939
Tune: John Foley, SJ, b.1939
© 1978, John B. Foley, SJ, and New Dawn Music. Published by OCP Publications.

## 243 Taste and See

Refrain

Taste and see, taste and see the good - ness of the
Lord. O taste and see, taste and see the
good - ness of the Lord, of the Lord.

Verses

1. I will bless the Lord at all times.
2. Glo - ri - fy the Lord with me.
3. Wor - ship the Lord, all you peo - ple.

Praise shall al - ways be on my lips;
To - geth - er let us all praise God's name.
You'll want for noth - ing if you ask.

my soul shall glo - ry in the Lord
I called the Lord who an - swered me;
Taste and see that the Lord is good;

for God has been so good to me.
from all my troub-les I was set free.
in God we need put all our trust.

Text: Psalm 34; James E. Moore, Jr., b.1951
Tune: James E. Moore, Jr., b.1951

## Let Us Talents and Tongues Employ 244

1. Let us tal - ents and tongues em - ploy,
2. Christ is a - ble to make us one,
3. Je - sus calls us in, sends us out

Reach - ing out with a
At the ta - ble he
Bear - ing fruit in a

shout of joy: Bread is bro - ken, the wine is poured,
sets the tone, Teach - ing peo - ple to live to bless,
world of doubt, Gives us love to tell, bread to share:

Christ is spo - ken and seen and heard.
Love in word and in deed ex - press.
God (Im - man - u - el) ev - 'ry - where!

Je - sus lives a - gain,

earth can breathe a - gain, pass the Word a - round: loaves a - bound!

Text: Fred Kaan, b.1929
Tune: LINSTEAD, LM with refrain; Jamaican folk tune, adapt. Doreen Potter, 1925-1980
© 1975, Hope Publishing Co.

## Rejoice in the Lord Always 245

Canon

Re - joice in the Lord al - ways, a - gain I say, re - joice! Re-

joice in the Lord al - ways, a - gain I say, re - joice! Re - joice! Re - joice! A-

*Last time*

gain I say, re - joice! Re - joice! Re - joice! A - gain I say, re - joice!

Text: Traditional
Tune: Traditional

## 246 When, in Our Music, God Is Glorified

1. When, in our mu - sic, God is glo - ri - fied,
2. How of - ten, mak - ing mu - sic, we have found
3. So has the Church, in lit - ur - gy and song,
4. And did not Je - sus sing a psalm that night
5. Let ev - 'ry in - stru-ment be tuned for praise!

And ad - o - ra - tion leaves no room for pride,
A new di - men - sion in the world of sound,
In faith and love, through cen - tu - ries of wrong,
When ut - most e - vil strove a - gainst the Light?
Let all re - joice who have a voice to raise!

It is as though the whole cre - a - tion cried:
As wor - ship moved us to a more pro - found
Borne wit - ness to the truth in ev - 'ry tongue: Al-le-lu -
Then let us sing, for whom he won the fight:
And may God give us faith to sing al - ways:

ia! Al-le-lu - ia! Al-le-lu - ia!

Text: Fred Pratt Green, 1903-2000, © 1972, Hope Publishing Co.
Tune: MAYFLOWER, 10 10 10 with alleluias; Marty Haugen, b.1950, © 1989, GIA Publications, Inc.

## 247 We Walk by Faith

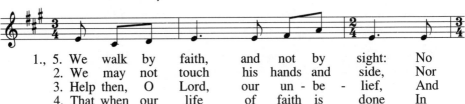

1., 5. We walk by faith, and not by sight: No
2. We may not touch his hands and side, Nor
3. Help then, O Lord, our un - be - lief, And
4. That when our life of faith is done In

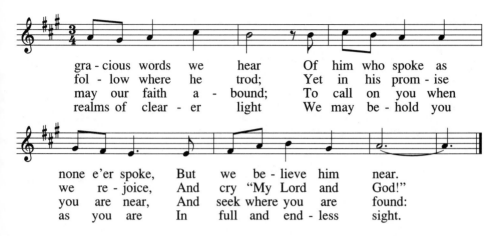

gra - cious words we hear Of him who spoke as
fol - low where he trod; Yet in his prom - ise
may our faith a - bound; To call on you when
realms of clear - er light We may be - hold you

none e'er spoke, But we be - lieve him near.
we re - joice, And cry "My Lord and God!"
you are near, And seek where you are found:
as you are In full and end - less sight.

Text: Henry Alford, 1810-1871, alt.
Tune: SHANTI, CM; Marty Haugen, b.1950, © 1984, GIA Publications, Inc.

## Prayer of Peace  248

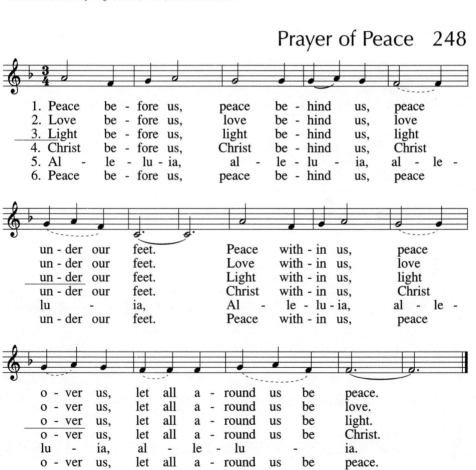

1. Peace be - fore us, peace be - hind us, peace
2. Love be - fore us, love be - hind us, love
3. Light be - fore us, light be - hind us, light
4. Christ be - fore us, Christ be - hind us, Christ
5. Al - le - lu - ia, al - le - lu - ia, al - le -
6. Peace be - fore us, peace be - hind us, peace

un - der our feet. Peace with - in us, peace
un - der our feet. Love with - in us, love
un - der our feet. Light with - in us, light
un - der our feet. Christ with - in us, Christ
lu - ia, Al - le - lu - ia, al - le -
un - der our feet. Peace with - in us, peace

o - ver us, let all a - round us be peace.
o - ver us, let all a - round us be love.
o - ver us, let all a - round us be light.
o - ver us, let all a - round us be Christ.
lu - ia, al - le - lu - ia.
o - ver us, let all a - round us be peace.

Text: Based on a Navajo prayer; David Haas, b.1957
Tune: David Haas, b.1957
© 1987, GIA Publications, Inc.

## 249   Soon and Very Soon

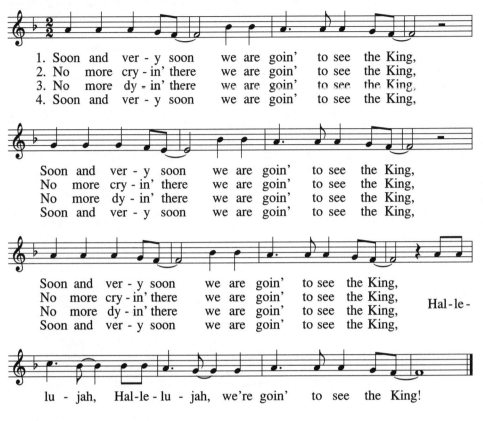

1. Soon and ver-y soon   we are goin'  to see  the King,
2. No   more cry-in' there   we are goin'  to see  the King,
3. No   more dy-in' there   we are goin'  to see  the King,
4. Soon and ver-y soon   we are goin'  to see  the King,

Soon and ver-y soon   we are goin'  to see  the King,
No   more cry-in' there   we are goin'  to see  the King,
No   more dy-in' there   we are goin'  to see  the King,
Soon and ver-y soon   we are goin'  to see  the King,

Soon and ver-y soon   we are goin'  to see  the King,
No   more cry-in' there   we are goin'  to see  the King,  Hal-le-
No   more dy-in' there   we are goin'  to see  the King,
Soon and ver-y soon   we are goin'  to see  the King,

lu - jah,  Hal-le-lu - jah, we're goin'  to  see  the King!

Text: Andraé Crouch
Tune: Andraé Crouch
© 1976, Bud John Songs, Inc./Crouch Music/ASCAP

## 250   Glory and Gratitude and Praise

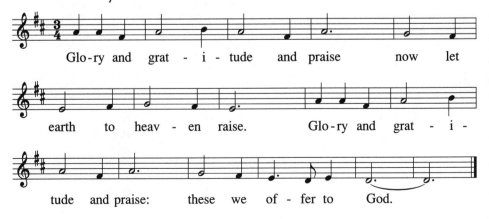

Glo-ry and  grat - i - tude   and praise   now   let

earth   to  heav - en  raise.   Glo-ry and  grat - i -

tude   and praise:   these  we   of - fer to   God.

Text: John L. Bell, b.1949
Tune: John L. Bell, b.1949
© 1994, Iona Community, GIA Publications, Inc., agent

# Over My Head   251

Text: African-American spiritual
Tune: African-American spiritual; arr. by John L. Bell, b.1949, © 1998, Iona Community, GIA Publications, Inc., agent

## 252 Shout for Joy

1. Shout for joy, loud and long, God be praised
2. By God's word all was made, Heav'n and earth,
3. Yet our pride makes us fall! So Christ came
4. Now has Christ tru - ly ris'n And his spir -
5. Rich and poor, we will sing, Hear - ing words
6. So we stand with our song! We will work

with a song! To the Lord we be - long— Chil - dren
light and shade, Na - ture's won - ders dis - played, We to
for us all— Not the right - eous to call— By his
it is giv'n To all those un - der heav'n Who will
that will ring, Bread and wine we will bring Here be -
all as one For the king - dom we long; We will

of our mak - er, God the great life - giv - er!
rule cre - a - tion From its first foun - da - tion.
cross and pas - sion, Bring - ing us sal - va - tion!
walk be - side him, Though they once de - nied him!
fore this ta - ble, With the weak and a - ble!
sing to - geth - er, With our God for - ev - er!

Shout for joy, joy, joy! Shout for joy, joy, joy!

God is love, God is light, God is ev - er - last - ing!

Text: Stanzas 1-4, David Mowbray, b.1938, © 1982, Jubilate Hymns, Ltd. (admin. by Hope Publishing Co.); stanzas 5-6, David Haas, b.1957,
© 1993, GIA Publications, Inc.
Tune: PERSONENT HODIE, 666 66 with refrain; *Piae Cantiones*, Griefswald, 1582; harm. by Diana Kodner, b.1957, © 1992, GIA Publications, Inc.

# Sing a New Song to the Lord 253

1. Sing a new song to the Lord, He to whom won-ders be-
long! Re-joice in his tri-umph and tell of his
power, O sing to the Lord a new song!

2. Now to the ends of the earth See his sal-va-tion is
shown; And still he re-mem-bers his mer-cy and
truth, Un-chang-ing in love to his own.

3. Sing a new song and re-joice, Pub-lish his prais-es a-
broad! Let voic-es in cho-rus, with trum-pet and
horn, Re-sound for the joy of the Lord!

4. Join with the hills and the sea Thun-ders of praise to pro-
long! In judg-ment and jus-tice he comes to the
earth, O sing to the Lord a new song!

Text: Psalm 98; Timothy Dudley-Smith, b.1926, © 1973, Hope Publishing Co.
Tune: CANTATE DOMINO (ONSLOW SQUARE), Irregular; David G. Wilson, b.1940, © 1973, Jubilate Hymns, Ltd. (admin. by Hope Publishing Co.)

# In the Lord I'll Be Ever Thankful 254

Ostinato Refrain

In the Lord I'll be ev-er thank-ful, in the Lord I will re-
joice! Look to God, do not be a-fraid; lift up your
voic-es, the Lord is near; lift up your voic-es, the Lord is near.

Text: Taizé Community
Tune: Jacques Berthier, 1923-1994
© 1986, 1991, Les Presses de Taizé, GIA Publications, Inc., agent

## 255 I Want to Walk as a Child of the Light

1. I want to walk as a child of the light.
2. I want to see the bright-ness of God.
3. I'm look-ing for the com-ing of Christ.

I want to fol - low Je - sus.
I want to look at Je - sus.
I want to be with Je - sus.

God set the stars to give light to the world. The
Clear sun of right-eous-ness shine on my path, And
When we have run with pa-tience the race, We

star of my life is Je - sus.
show me the way to the Fa - ther.
shall know the joy of Je - sus.

In him there is no dark - ness at all. The

night and the day are both a - like. The

Lamb is the light of the cit - y of God.

Shine in my heart, Lord Je - sus.

Text: Ephesians 5:8-10, Revelation 21:23, John 12:46, 1 John 1:5, Hebrews 12:1; Kathleen Thomerson, b.1934, © 1970, 1975, Celebration
Tune: HOUSTON, 10 7 10 8 9 9 11 7; Kathleen Thomerson, b.1934, © 1970, 1975, Celebration; acc. by Robert J. Batastini, b.1942, © 1987, GIA
    Publications, Inc.

# Joyful, Joyful, We Adore You  256

1. Joy - ful, joy - ful, we a - dore you, God of glo - ry,
2. All your works with joy sur - round you, Earth and heav'n re -
3. Al - ways giv - ing and for - giv - ing, Ev - er bless - ing,
4. Mor - tals join the might - y cho - rus, Which the morn - ing

Lord of love; Hearts un - fold like flowers be - fore you,
flect your rays, Stars and an - gels sing a - round you,
ev - er blest, Well - spring of the joy of liv - ing,
stars be - gan; God's own love is reign - ing o'er us,

Open - ing to the sun a - bove. Melt the clouds of
Cen - ter of un - bro - ken praise; Field and for - est,
O - cean depth of hap - py rest! Lov - ing Fa - ther,
Join - ing peo - ple hand in hand. Ev - er sing - ing,

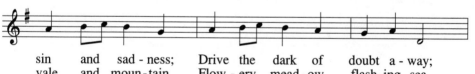

sin and sad - ness; Drive the dark of doubt a - way;
vale and moun - tain, Flow - ery mead - ow, flash - ing sea,
Christ our broth - er, Let your light up - on us shine;
march we on - ward, Vic - tors in the midst of strife;

Giv - er of im - mor - tal glad - ness, Fill us with the light of day!
Chant - ing bird and flow - ing foun - tain, Prais - ing you e - ter - nal - ly!
Teach us how to love each oth - er, Lift us to the joy di - vine.
Joy - ful mu - sic leads us sun - ward In the tri - umph song of life.

Text: Henry van Dyke, 1852-1933, alt.
Tune: HYMN TO JOY, 8 7 8 7 D; arr. from Ludwig van Beethoven, 1770-1827, by Edward Hodges, 1796-1867

## 257 Alabaré

Refrain

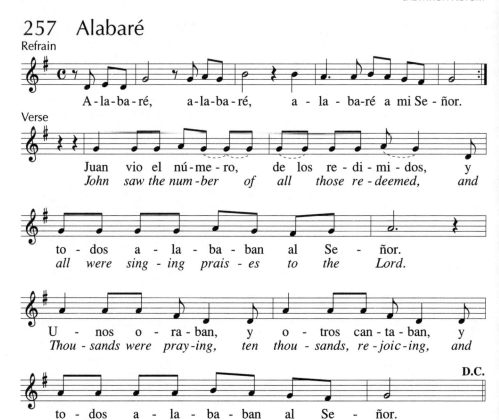

A-la-ba-ré, a-la-ba-ré, a - la - ba-ré a mi Se - ñor.

Verse

Juan vio el nú-me-ro, de los re - di - mi - dos, y
*John saw the num-ber of all those re-deemed, and*

to - dos a - la - ba-ban al Se - ñor.
*all were sing - ing prais - es to the Lord.*

U - nos o - ra - ban, y o - tros can-ta-ban, y
*Thou - sands were pray-ing, ten thou - sands, re-joic-ing, and*

D.C.

to - dos a - la - ba - ban al Se - ñor.
*all were sing - ing prais - es to the Lord.*

Text: *I will praise the Lord;* Manuel José Alonso, José Pagán; trans. unknown
Tune: Manuel José Alonso, José Pagán; acc. by Diana Kodner, b.1957
© 1979, Manuel José Alonso, José Pagán, and Ediciones Musical PAX. Published by OCP Publications.

## 258 If You Believe and I Believe

If you be - lieve and I be - lieve And we to-geth - er

pray, The Ho - ly Spir - it must come down And

set God's peo - ple free, And set God's peo - ple

free, And set God's peo - ple free; The

Ho - ly Spir - it must come down And set God's peo - ple free.

Text: Zimbabwean traditional
Tune: Zimbabwean traditional; adapt. of English traditional; as taught by Tarasai; arr. by John L. Bell, b.1949, © 1991, Iona Community,
    GIA Publications, Inc., agent

## Lift High the Cross  259

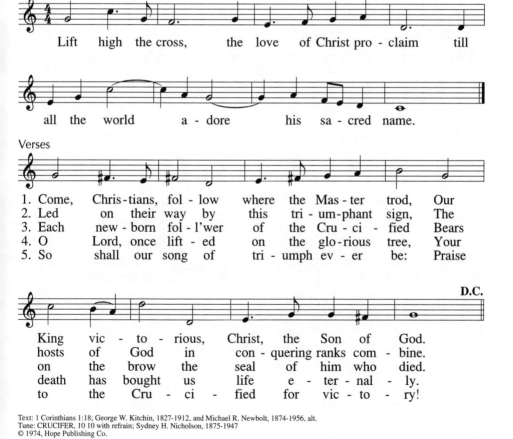

**Refrain**

Lift high the cross, the love of Christ pro - claim till

all the world a - dore his sa - cred name.

**Verses**

1. Come, Chris-tians, fol - low where the Mas - ter trod, Our
2. Led on their way by this tri - um-phant sign, The
3. Each new - born fol - l'wer of the Cru - ci - fied Bears
4. O Lord, once lift - ed on the glo-rious tree, Your
5. So shall our song of tri - umph ev - er be: Praise

**D.C.**

King vic - to - rious, Christ, the Son of God.
hosts of God in con - quering ranks com - bine.
on the brow the seal of him who died.
death has bought us life e - ter - nal - ly.
to the Cru - ci - fied for vic - to - ry!

Text: 1 Corinthians 1:18; George W. Kitchin, 1827-1912, and Michael R. Newbolt, 1874-1956, alt.
Tune: CRUCIFER, 10 10 with refrain; Sydney H. Nicholson, 1875-1947
© 1974, Hope Publishing Co.

# 260 Freedom Is Coming

O Jesus, O Jesus,
O Jesus, Jesus is coming,
O yes, I know,

Text: South African
Tune: South African
© 1984, Utryck, Walton Music Corporation, agent

# Lord of All Hopefulness   261

1. Lord of all hope - ful - ness, Lord of all joy,
2. Lord of all ea - ger - ness, Lord of all faith,
3. Lord of all kind - li - ness, Lord of all grace,
4. Lord of all gen - tle - ness, Lord of all calm,

Whose trust, ev - er child - like, no cares can de - stroy,
Whose strong hands were skilled at the plane and the lathe,
Your hands swift to wel - come, your arms to em - brace,
Whose voice is con - tent - ment, whose pres - ence is balm,

Be there at our wak - ing, and give us, we pray,
Be there at our la - bors, and give us, we pray,
Be there at our hom - ing, and give us, we pray,
Be there at our sleep - ing, and give us, we pray,

Your bliss in our hearts, Lord, at the break of the day.
Your strength in our hearts, Lord, at the noon of the day.
Your love in our hearts, Lord, at the eve of the day.
Your peace in our hearts, Lord, at the end of the day.

Text: Jan Struther, 1901-1953, © Oxford University Press
Tune: SLANE, 10 11 11 12; Gaelic; harm. by Erik Routley, 1917-1982, © 1975, Hope Publishing Co.

# We Are Walking in the Light   262

We are walk-ing in the light, in the light, in the light.

We are walk-ing in the light, in the light of God.

Text: Traditional
Tune: James Moore, Jr., © 1987, GIA Publications, Inc.

## 263 Amazing Grace

1. A - maz - ing grace! how sweet the sound, That
2. 'Twas grace that taught my heart to fear, And
3. The Lord has prom - ised good to me, His
4. Through man - y dan - gers, toils, and snares, I
5. When we've been there ten thou - sand years, Bright

saved a wretch like me! I once was lost, but
grace my fears re - lieved; How pre - cious did that
word my hope se - cures; He will my shield and
have al - read - y come; 'Tis grace has brought me
shin - ing as the sun, We've no less days to

now am found, Was blind, but now I see.
grace ap - pear The hour I first be - lieved!
por - tion be As long as life en - dures.
safe thus far, And grace will lead me home.
sing God's praise Than when we'd first be - gun.

Text: St. 1-4, John Newton, 1725-1807; st. 5, attr. to John Rees, fl.1859
Tune: NEW BRITAIN, CM; *Virginia Harmony*, 1831; harm. by John Barnard, b.1948, © 1982, Jubilate Hymns, Ltd. (admin. by Hope Publishing Co.)

## 264 Behold, I Make All Things New

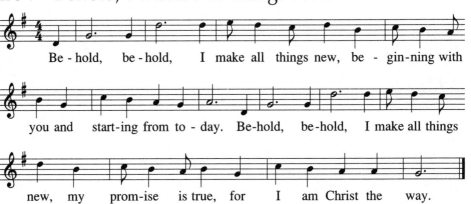

Be - hold, be - hold, I make all things new, be - gin-ning with

you and start-ing from to - day. Be-hold, be-hold, I make all things

new, my prom-ise is true, for I am Christ the way.

Text: John L. Bell, b.1949
Tune: John L. Bell, b.1949
© 1994, The Iona Community, GIA Publications, Inc., agent

# Walk, Walk In the Light  265

Verses

Cantor:

1. ⁷ Je - sus is the Light for all:
2. The light of Je - sus is yours and mine:
3. We walk to - geth - er in Je - sus' light:
4. ⁷ Je - sus leads us on our way:

All:

Walk, walk in the light!

Cantor:

⁷ we fol - low him as we
⁷ nev - er to hide it but to
and let our own light
we help each oth - er each and

All:

hear his call.
let it shine.
shine so bright.   Walk, walk in the light!
ev - 'ry day.

Refrain

Walk, walk in the light!   Walk, walk in the light!

1.-3.

Walk, walk in the light;   walk in the light of the Lord!

D.C. | 4. | *To refrain* | Final ending

Lord!   Lord!

Text: Traditional; verses by Carey Landry, © 1996
Tune: Traditional; arr. by Carey Landry and Jeophry Scott, acc. by Carl Rutterson, © 1996, Carey Landry
Published by OCP Publications.

# 266 Ave Maria

Verses

1. Hail Mar - y full of grace, the
2. Ho - ly Mar - y moth-er of God, the

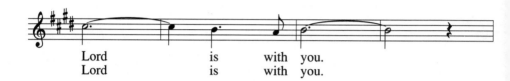

Lord is with you.
Lord is with you.

Bless - ed are you a - mong all wom-en,
Pray for us sin - ners, pray for us sin - ners,

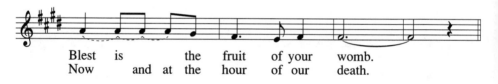

Blest is the fruit of your womb.
Now and at the hour of our death.

Refrain

Je - sus, formed in your faith, A - ve Ma - ri - a al - le -

lu - ia. Je - sus, born in your love,

A - ve Ma - ri - a al - le - lu - ia.

Text: Hail Mary; additional text by Dan Kantor, b.1960
Tune: Dan Kantor, b.1960; arr. by Rob Glover
© 1993, GIA Publications, Inc.

# Sing of Mary, Meek and Lowly    267

1. Sing of Mar - y meek and low - ly, Vir - gin - moth - er
2. Sing of Je - sus, son of Mar - y, In the home at
3. Glo - ry be to God the Fa - ther; Glo - ry be to

pure and mild, Sing of God's own Son most ho - ly,
Naz - a - reth. Toil and la - bor can - not wea - ry
God the Son; Glo - ry be to God the Spir - it;

Who be - came her lit - tle child. Fair - est child of
Love en - dur - ing un - to death. Con - stant was the
Glo - ry to the Three in One. From the heart of

fair - est moth-er, God the Lord who came to earth,
love he gave her, Though he went forth from her side,
bless - ed Mar - y, From all saints the song as - cends,

Word made flesh, our ver - y broth - er,
Forth to preach, and heal, and suf - fer,
And the church the strain re - ech - oes

Takes our na - ture by his birth.
Till on Cal - va - ry he died.
Un - to earth's re - mot - est ends.

Text: Roland F. Palmer, 1891-1985
Tune: PLEADING SAVIOR, 8 7 8 7 D; *Christian Lyre*, 1830; harm. by Richard Proulx, b.1937, © 1986, GIA Publications, Inc.

# 268 Magnificat / Sing Out, My Soul

Canon

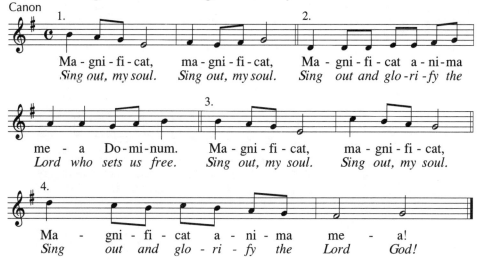

Ma - gni - fi - cat, ma - gni - fi - cat, Ma - gni - fi - cat a - ni - ma
*Sing out, my soul.* *Sing out, my soul.* *Sing out and glo -ri -fy the*

me - a Do - mi - num. Ma - gni - fi - cat, ma - gni - fi - cat,
*Lord who sets us free.* *Sing out, my soul.* *Sing out, my soul.*

Ma - gni - fi - cat a - ni - ma me - a!
*Sing out and glo -ri - fy the Lord God!*

Text: Luke 1:46, *My soul magnifies the Lord;* Taizé Community, 1978
Tune: Jacques Berthier, 1923-1994
© 1979, Les Presses de Taizé, GIA Publications, Inc., agent

# 269 Holy Is Your Name

Refrain

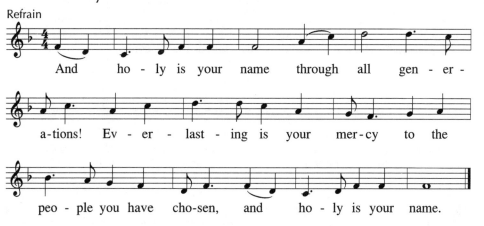

And ho - ly is your name through all gen - er -

a -tions! Ev - er - last - ing is your mer-cy to the

peo - ple you have cho-sen, and ho - ly is your name.

Verses

1. My soul is filled with joy as I sing to God my savior:
   you have looked upon your servant, you have visited your people.

2. I am lowly as a child, but I know from this day forward
   that my name will be remembered, for all will call me blessed.

3. I proclaim the pow'r of God, you do marvels for your servants;
   though you scatter the proud hearted, and destroy the might of princes.

4. To the hungry you give food, send the rich away empty.
In your mercy you are mindful of the people you have chosen.

5. In your love you now fulfill what you promised to your people.
I will praise you, Lord, my savior, everlasting is your mercy.

Text: Luke 1:46-55, David Haas, b.1957
Tune: WILD MOUNTAIN THYME, Irregular; Irish traditional; arr. by David Haas, b.1957
© 1989, GIA Publications, Inc.

## Immaculate Mary    270

1. Im - mac - u - late Mar - y, your prais - es we sing;
2. Pre - des - tined for Christ by e - ter - nal de - cree,
3. To you by an an - gel, the Lord God made known
4. Most blest of all wom - en, you heard and be - lieved,
5. The an - gels re - joiced when you brought forth God's Son;

You reign now in splen - dor with Je - sus our King.
God willed you both vir - gin and moth - er to be.
The grace of the Spir - it, the gift of the Son.
Most blest in the fruit of your womb then con - ceived.
Your joy is the joy of all a - ges to come.

A - ve, A - ve, A - ve, Ma - ri - a.

A - ve, A - ve, Ma - ri - a.

6. Your child is the Savior, all hope lies in him:
He gives us new life and redeems us from sin.

7. In glory for ever now close to your Son,
All ages will praise you for all God has done.

Text: St. 1, Jeremiah Cummings, 1814-1866, alt.; St. 2-7, Brian Foley, b.1919, © 1971, Faber Music Ltd.
Tune: LOURDES HYMN, 11 11 with refrain; Grenoble, 1882

## 271 Jerusalem, My Happy Home

1. Je - ru - sa - lem, my hap - py home, When
2. Your saints are crowned with glo - ry great; They
3. There Da - vid stands with harp in hand As
4. Our La - dy sings Mag - nif - i - cat With
5. There Mag - da - lene has left her tears, And
6. Je - ru - sa - lem, Je - ru - sa - lem, God

shall I with you be? When shall my sor - rows
see God face to face; They tri - umph still, they
mas - ter of the choir: Ten thou - sand times that
tune sur - pass - ing sweet; And all the vir - gins
cheer - ful - ly does sing With bless - ed saints, whose
grant that I may see Your end - less joy, and

have an end? Your joys when shall I see?
still re - joice: In that most ho - ly place.
we were blest That might this mu - sic hear.
join the song While sit - ting at her feet.
har - mo - ny In ev - 'ry street does ring.
of the same Par - tak - er ev - er be!

Text: Joseph Bromehead, 1747-1826, alt.
Tune: LAND OF REST, CM; American; harm. by Richard Proulx, b.1937, © 1975, GIA Publications, Inc.

## 272 Christ Is the King

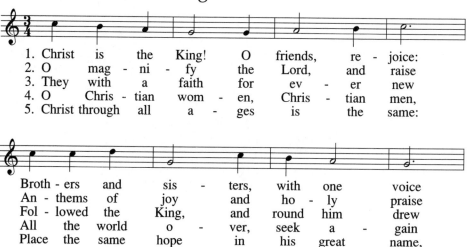

1. Christ is the King! O friends, re - joice:
2. O mag - ni - fy the Lord, and raise
3. They with a faith for ev - er new
4. O Chris - tian wom - en, Chris - tian men,
5. Christ through all a - ges is the same:

Broth - ers and sis - ters, with one voice
An - thems of joy and ho - ly praise
Fol - lowed the King, and round him drew
All the world o - ver, seek a - gain
Place the same hope in his great name,

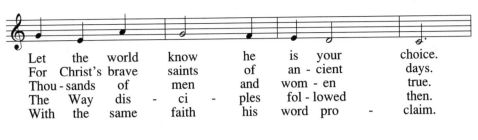

Let    the    world    know    he    is    your    choice.
For    Christ's    brave    saints    of    an - cient    days.
Thou - sands    of    men    and    wom - en    true.
The    Way    dis - ci - ples    fol - lowed    then.
With    the    same    faith    his    word    pro - claim.

Al - le - lu - ia,    al - le - lu - ia,    al - le - lu - ia.

Text: George K. A. Bell, 1883-1958, alt., © Oxford University Press
Tune: GELOBT SEI GOTT, 888 with alleluias; Melchior Vulpius, c.1560-1616

## All Night, All Day   273

Refrain

All    night,    all    day,    an - gels    watch - ing    o - ver    me,    my    Lord.

All    night,    all    day,    an - gels    watch - ing    o - ver    me.

Verses

1. Now    I    lay    me    down    to    sleep.
2. Lord,    stay    with    me    through    the    night.

An - gels    watch - ing    o - ver    me,    my    Lord.    Pray    the    Lord    my
An - gels    watch - ing    o - ver    me,    my    Lord.    Wake    me    with    the

D.C.

soul    will    keep.    An - gels    watch - ing    o - ver    me.
morn - ing    light.    An - gels    watch - ing    o - ver    me.

Text: African-American traditional
Tune: ALL NIGHT, ALL DAY, 7 9 7 7 with refrain; African-American traditional; acc. by Robert J. Batastini, b.1942, © 2000, GIA Publications, Inc.

# 274 We Sing of the Saints

1. We sing of the saints filled with Spir-it and grace, Blest wom-en and
2. *(Optional verse for saint's day)*
3. We, too, have been cho-sen to fol-low the way Of good-ness and

men through all time, from each place. God chose them, the ho - ly, the

truth in our stud - y and play, We raise up our song, liv - ing

hum - ble, the wise To spread the Good News of sal - va - tion in Christ.

saints here be - low, With heav - en - ly saints, as our praise ev - er flows.

## Optional Verses for Saint's Days

2. **Feasts of Mary**
A lowly, young woman God's mother would be,
The first true believing disciple was she.
From cradle to cross, she would follow her Son
And share in the life everlasting he won.

**Feasts of Joseph**
A carpenter, upright and faithful, was called
To care for young Jesus, a child weak and small.
To teach and to guide, to embrace him in love,
Reminding him here of the Father above.

**Feasts of John the Baptist**
A prophet and herald who made straight the way
For Jesus to come, bringing mercy's new day.
He preached to the people to change and repent,
Preparing them as the Messiah was sent.

**St. Patrick (March 17)**
From Britain to Ireland strong Patrick returned,
He baptized and preached in the name of our Lord.
He used simple clover to show God was One,
To teach of the Father and Spirit and Son.

**Blessed Kateri Tekakwitha (July 14)**
The "Lily of Mohawks," Kateri was called
For sharing God's love with the great and the small,
She bore the name "Christian" with honor and pride,
And now her name, "Blessed" is known far and wide.

### St. Augustine (August 28)
A great, holy man, born on Africa's shores
Augustine, at first, loved the worldly life more;
He found later on, Jesus Christ, the true Way,
And chose the true Gospel to live and proclaim.

### Archangels (September 29)
Of Gabriel, Raphael, Michael we sing,
God's messengers; joyful, glad tidings they bring;
Protecting the Church, and announcing the time
When Christ shall return in his glory sublime.

### St. Francis of Assisi (October 4)
Saint Francis was born a rich, noble young man,
But God had in mind a much different plan;
So Francis left status and money behind,
To help many people God's true will to find.

### St. Teresa of Jesus (October 15)
A woman of wisdom, of faith and of prayer,
Teresa would speak up when others didn't dare.
She challenged the Church to renew and revive;
Her great love of Jesus was always her guide.

### All Saints (November 1)
There are many saints whom we don't know by name,
For God works through people who never find fame.
But, gathered together, they now sing God's might,
With martyrs and prophets, in heavenly light.

### All Souls (November 2)
We honor the mem'ry of those now at rest,
Who followed the Gospel, whose lives were so blest;
From fam'lies and friendships, they make heaven seem
More home-like for us, in our prayers and our dreams.

### St. Nicholas (December 6)
A bishop, a friend of the poor and the weak,
Of orphans and children, the hungry, the meek;
To help those in need, to return them to health,
Saint Nicholas used all his power and wealth.

### Blessed Juan Diego (December 9)
This poor Aztec native lived in Mexico;
Was given a sign: roses blooming in snow.
The Mother of God to Diego appeared,
So Jesus her Son would be always revered.

### St. Lucy (December 13)
Her feast is in Advent, her name means "the light,"
She died for upholding what she thought was right;
St. Lucy took care of the poor and the frail;
Her witness was brave and her faith never failed.

Text: Alan J. Hommerding, b.1956, © 1994, World Library Publications, Inc.
Tune: ZIE GINDS KOMT DE STOOMBOOT, 11 11 11 11; Traditional Dutch melody; acc. by Karl A. Pölm-Faudré, © 1984

# 275 Blessed Feasts of Blessed Martyrs

1. Bless - ed feasts of bless - ed mar - tyrs, Ho - ly wom - en,
2. Faith pre - vail - ing, hope un - fail - ing, Lov - ing Christ with
3. There - fore, all that reign in glo - ry, Strong and sure with

ho - ly men, With our love and ad - mi - ra - tion,
sin - gle heart, Thus they, glo - rious and vic - to - rious,
Christ on high, Join to ours your sup - pli - ca - tion

Greet we your re - turn a - gain. Wor - thy deeds are
Brave - ly bore the mar - tyr's part, By con - tempt of
When be - fore him we draw nigh, Pray - ing that, this

theirs, and won - ders, Wor - thy of the name they bore;
ev - 'ry an - guish, By un - yield - ing bat - tle done;
life com - plet - ed, All its fleet - ing mo - ments past,

We, with joy - ful praise and sing - ing,
Vic - tors at the last, they tri - umph,
By his grace we may be wor - thy

Hon - or them for ev - er - more.
With the host of an - gels one.
Of e - ter - nal bliss at last.

Text: *O beata beatorum*, Latin, 12th. C.; tr. John M. Neale, 1818-1866, alt.
Tune: HYMN TO JOY, 8 7 8 7 D; arr. from Ludwig van Beethoven, 1770-1827, by Edward Hodges, 1796-1867

# We See the Lord   276

1. We   see the Lord,   we   see the Lord,   and he   is
2. We   see the Lord,   we   see the Lord,   ᵧ and God's
3. We   hear the Lord,   we   hear the Lord,   ᵧ and God's
4. We   bless the Lord,   we   bless the Lord,   ᵧ and as

high and lift - ed   up,   and his   train   fills   the Tem-ple, he   is
face   shines   forth   as   a   light   in   the Tem-ple, and God's
Word   is - sues forth   and re - sounds through the Tem-ple, and God's
in - cense goes up,   so our prayers   fill   the Tem-ple, and as

high and lift - ed   up,   and his   train   fills   the Tem-ple.   The
face   shines   forth   as   a   light   in   the Tem-ple.   The
Word   is - sues forth   and re - sounds through the Tem-ple.   The
in - cense goes up,   so our prayers   fill   the Tem-ple.   The

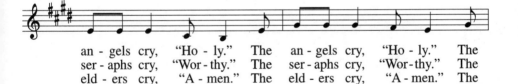

an - gels cry,   "Ho - ly."   The   an - gels cry,   "Ho - ly."   The
ser - aphs cry,   "Wor - thy."   The   ser - aphs cry,   "Wor-thy."   The
eld - ers cry,   "A - men."   The   eld - ers cry,   "A - men."   The
peo - ple cry,   "Glo - ry."   The   peo - ple cry,   "Glo - ry."   The

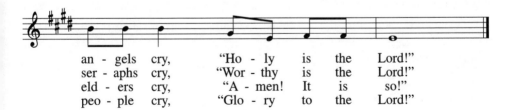

an - gels   cry,   "Ho - ly   is   the   Lord!"
ser - aphs   cry,   "Wor - thy   is   the   Lord!"
eld - ers   cry,   "A - men!   It   is   so!"
peo - ple   cry,   "Glo - ry   to   the   Lord!"

Text: Vs. 1, Isaiah 6:1-3; vss. 2-4, James E. Byrne, © 1973
Tune: Traditional; arr. by Charles High, © 1978, The Word of God Music; acc. by Robert J. Batastini, b.1942, © 1989, GIA Publications, Inc.

# 277 Chatter with the Angels

*Chat-ter with the an - gels soon in the morn - ing.

Chat - ter with the an - gels in that land.

Chat - ter with the an - gels soon in the morn - ing.

Chat - ter with the an - gels, join the band.

I hope to join that band and Chat-ter with the an - gels

all day long! I hope to join that band and

Chat - ter with the an - gels all day long!

\* *March* with the angels.
*Skip* with the angels.
*Dance* with the angels.
*Tiptoe* with the angels.

Text: African-American traditional
Tune: African-American traditional; acc. by Robert J. Batastini, b.1942, © 2000, GIA Publications, Inc.

## Good Morning, God 278

1. Good morn - ing, God, the night is gone.
2. God, grant that in the morn - ing light

We bring to you a morn - ing song.
We see things clear - ly and a - right.

Now chase the shades of night a - way
God, as we greet this fresh new day

And turn the dark - ness in - to day.
Take an - ger, fear, and doubt a - way.

Text: Ken Medema, alt., © 1988, Brier Patch Music
Tune: O WALY WALY, LM; English traditional; acc. by Robert J. Batastini, b.1942, © 2000, GIA Publications, Inc.

## Morning Has Broken 279

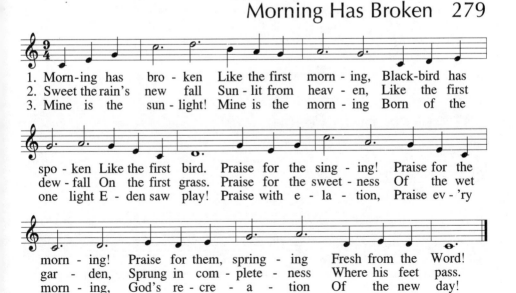

1. Morn - ing has bro - ken Like the first morn - ing, Black-bird has
2. Sweet the rain's new fall Sun - lit from heav - en, Like the first
3. Mine is the sun - light! Mine is the morn - ing Born of the

spo - ken Like the first bird. Praise for the sing - ing! Praise for the
dew - fall On the first grass. Praise for the sweet - ness Of the wet
one light E - den saw play! Praise with e - la - tion, Praise ev - 'ry

morn - ing! Praise for them, spring - ing Fresh from the Word!
gar - den, Sprung in com - plete - ness Where his feet pass.
morn - ing, God's re - cre - a - tion Of the new day!

Text: Eleanor Farjeaon, 1881-1965, *The Children's Bells*, © David Higham Assoc. Ltd.
Tune: BUNESSAN, 5 5 5 4 D; Gaelic; acc. by Robert J. Batastini, b.1942, © 1999, GIA Publications, Inc.

# 280  At Evening

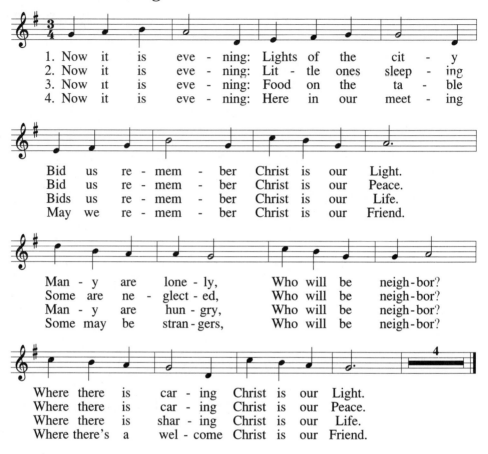

1. Now it is eve - ning: Lights of the cit - y
2. Now it is eve - ning: Lit - tle ones sleep - ing
3. Now it is eve - ning: Food on the ta - ble
4. Now it is eve - ning: Here in our meet - ing

Bid us re - mem - ber Christ is our Light.
Bid us re - mem - ber Christ is our Peace.
Bids us re - mem - ber Christ is our Life.
May we re - mem - ber Christ is our Friend.

Man - y are lone - ly, Who will be neigh-bor?
Some are ne - glect - ed, Who will be neigh-bor?
Man - y are hun - gry, Who will be neigh-bor?
Some may be stran - gers, Who will be neigh-bor?

Where there is car - ing Christ is our Light.
Where there is car - ing Christ is our Peace.
Where there is shar - ing Christ is our Life.
Where there's a wel - come Christ is our Friend.

Text: Fred Pratt Green, 1903-2000, © 1974, Hope Publishing Co.
Tune: EVENING HYMN, 5 5 5 4 D; David Haas, b.1957, © 1985, GIA Publications, Inc.

# 281  Go Now in Peace

Canon

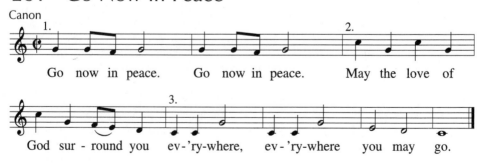

Go now in peace. Go now in peace. May the love of

God sur - round you ev-'ry-where, ev-'ry-where you may go.

Text: Natalie Sleeth, 1930-1992
Tune: Natalie Sleeth, 1930-1992; acc. by Robert J. Batastini, b.1942
© 1976, Hinshaw Music, Inc.

## Song of St. Patrick 282

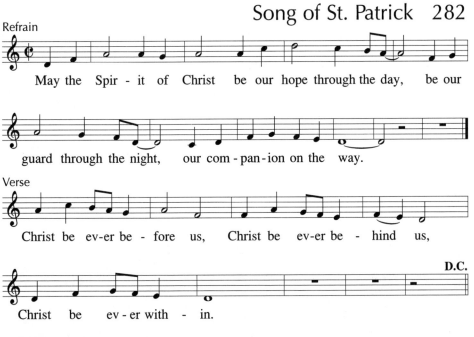

Refrain

May the Spir-it of Christ be our hope through the day, be our guard through the night, our com-pan-ion on the way.

Verse

Christ be ev-er be-fore us, Christ be ev-er be-hind us, Christ be ev-er with-in.

D.C.

Text: Based on *St. Patrick's Breastplate;* Marty Haugen, b.1950
Tune: Marty Haugen, b.1950
© 1986, GIA Publications, Inc.

## May the Lord, Mighty God 283

1., 3. May the Lord, might-y God, bless and keep you for-ev - er, grant you peace, per - fect peace, cour-age in ev - 'ry en - deav - or.

2. Lift your eyes and see God's face full of grace for - ev - er. May the Lord, might-y God, bless and keep you for-ev - er.

Text: Numbers 6:24-26; unknown
Tune: WEN-TI, Irregular; Chinese, Pao-chen Li; adapted by I-to Loh, © 1983, Abingdon Press; acc. by Diana Kodner, b.1957, © 1993,
  GIA Publications, Inc.

## 284 Amen Siakudumisa / Amen, We Praise Your Name

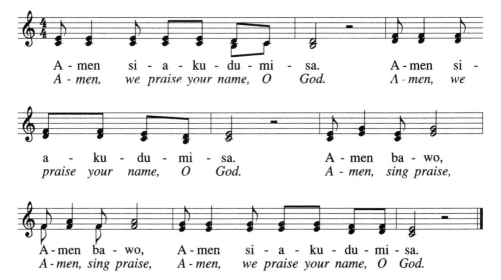

A - men si - a - ku - du - mi - sa.
*A - men, we praise your name, O God.*

A - men si -
*A - men, we*

a - ku - du - mi - sa.
*praise your name, O God.*

A - men ba - wo,
*A - men, sing praise,*

A - men ba - wo,
*A - men, sing praise,*

A - men
*A - men,*

si - a - ku - du - mi - sa.
*we praise your name, O God.*

Text: *Amen. Praise the name of the Lord.* South African traditional
Tune: Attributed to S.C. Molefe as taught by George Mxadana; arr. by John L. Bell, b.1949, © 1990, Iona Community, GIA Publications, Inc., agent

## 285 For Your Gracious Blessing

Canon

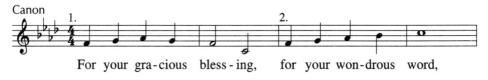

For your gra-cious bless-ing, for your won-drous word,

for your lov-ing kind-ness, we give thanks, O God.

Text: Traditional
Tune: Traditional; acc. by Robert N. Roth, © 2000, GIA Publications, Inc.

## 286 For Health and Strength

Canon

1. For health and strength and dai-ly food,
2. For neigh-bors, friends, and fam-i-ly, We give you thanks, O God.
3. For faith and hope and lov-ing care,

Text: Vs. 1, traditional; vss. 2-3, Bert Polman, © 1994, CRC Publications
Tune: FOR HEALTH AND STRENGTH, 8 6; Anonymous; acc. by Robert J. Batastini, b.1942, © 2000, GIA Publications, Inc.

# Final Blessing  287

May God bless and keep us, may God smile on us.

May God show us kind - ness, fill us with peace.

And may God bless us, Fa - ther, Son, and Spir - it;

May we al - ways love and serve, filled with God's peace.

Text: Numbers 6:24-26; David Haas, b.1957, © 1997, GIA Publications, Inc.
Tune: ADORO TE DEVOTE; Mode V; adapt. by David Haas, b.1957, © 1997, GIA Publications, Inc.

## SERVICE MUSIC

All music found from nos. 9 to 97 is copyright by GIA Publications, Inc., with the exception of those items specified below. Please refer to nos. 9 to 97 for specific copyright dates.

**2** Text: © 1969, James Quinn, SJ. Used by permission of Selah Publishing Co., Inc., Kingston, NY 12401, North American agent. www.selahpub.com. All rights reserved. Acc.: © 1999, GIA Publications, Inc.

**3** Text. © 1963, 1993, The Grail, GIA Publications, Inc., agent. Tune: © 1990, GIA Publications, Inc.

**4** Text: © 1992, GIA Publications, Inc. Tune: © 1987, GIA Publicatins, Inc.

**6** Text: © 1969, James Quinn, SJ. Used by permission of Selah Publishing Co., Inc., Kingston, NY 12401, North American agent. www.selahpub.com. All rights reserved.

**7** © 1988, GIA Publications, Inc.

**8** Text: © 1992, GIA Publications, Inc. Harm.: From *The English Hymnal,* © Oxford University Press

**60** Trans.: © 1989, The United Methodist Publishing House (Administered by THE COPYRIGHT COMPANY, Nashville, TN) All Rights Reserved. International Copyright Secured. Used By Permission.

**66** Music: © 1973, 1979, GIA Publications, Inc. Tone for verses: © 1978, Augsburg Fortress

**98** Acc.: © 1975, GIA Publications, Inc.

**99** Text: © David Higham Assoc., Ltd. Harm.: From *The Oxford Book of Carols,* © Oxford University Press

**100** © 1984, Augsburg Fortress

**101** © 1984, Les Presses de Taizé, GIA Publications, Inc., agent

**102** © 1997, GIA Publications, Inc.

**103** © 1988, 1989, 1990, Christopher Walker. Published by OCP Publications. P.O. Box 13248, Portland, OR 97213-0248. All rights reserved. Used with permission.

**104** © 1994, Les Presses de Taizé, GIA Publications, Inc., agent

**105** © 1982, GIA Publications, Inc.

**107** Tune: © 1979, 1988, Les Presses de Taizé, GIA Publications, Inc., agent

**109** © 1984, GIA Publications, Inc.

**110** Harm.: © 1994, GIA Publications, Inc.

**111** Tune tr. and arr.: © 1990, Iona Community, GIA Publications, Inc., agent

**114** Text: Adapt. © Mrs. John W. Work III. Harm.: © 1995, GIA Publications, Inc.

**115** Harm.: © 1961, General Convention of the Episcopal Church, USA. Reprinted with the permission of the Domestic and Foreign Missionary Society of the Protestant Episcopal Church, USA

**116** Text and tune: © 1945, Boosey and Co., Ltd. Copyright Renewed. Reprinted by permission of Boosey and Hawkes, Inc. Acc.: © 1993, GIA Publications, Inc.

**118** Acc.: © 2000, GIA Publications, Inc.

**120** Text: © 1989, Hope Publishing Co., Carol Stream, IL 60188. All rights reserved. Used by permission. Tune: © 1991, GIA Publications, Inc.

**121** Text trans.: © Peter J. Scagnelli

**122** © 1981, Les Presses de Taizé, GIA Publications, Inc., agent.

**123** Text trans.: © Peter J. Scagnelli. Acc.: © 1975, GIA Publications, Inc.

**124** Acc.: © 2000, GIA Publications, Inc.

**125** Harm.: © 1987, GIA Publications, Inc.

**126** Harm.: From *Cantate Domino,* © 1980, World Council of Churches

**127** © 1953, copyright renewed, Doris M. Akers. All rights administered by Unichappell Music, Inc. International Copyright Secured. All rights reserved.

**128** © 1983, GIA Publications, Inc.

**129** © 1990, 1991, GIA Publications, Inc.

**130** © 1982, Les Presses de Taizé, GIA Publications, Inc., agent

**131** © 1969, Hope Publishing Co., Carol Stream, IL 60188. All rights reserved. Used by permission.

**132** © 1973, Word of God Music (Administered by THE COPYRIGHT COMPANY, Nashville, TN) All Rights Reserved. International Copyright Secured. Used By Permission.

**133** © 1984, Les Presses de Taizé, GIA Publications, Inc., agent

**134** © 1979, Les Presses de Taizé, GIA Publications, Inc., agent

**135** Text and acc.: © 1978, 1990, Les Presses de Taizé, GIA Publications, Inc., agent

**136** © 1982, 1991, 1997, GIA Publications, Inc.

**137** © 1986, GIA Publications, Inc.

**138** © 1988, 1989, Christopher Walker. Published by OCP Publications. P.O. Box 13248, Portland, OR 97213-0248. All rights reserved. Used with permission.

**139** Text: © 2001, GIA Publications, Inc. Acc.: © 2000, GIA Publications, Inc.

**144** Text tr.: © J. Curwen and Sons. Harm.: From *The English Hymnal,* © Oxford University Press

**145** © 1980, GIA Publications, Inc.

**147** Text and tune: © 1977, Patricia Joyce Shelly. Acc.: © 2000, GIA Publications, Inc.

**148** Text: St. 2-3, © 1987, CRC Publications, Grand Rapids, MI 49650. All rights reserved. Used by permission. Acc.: © 2000, GIA Publications, Inc.

**150** © 1968, Augsburg Fortress

**151** Acc.: © 1984, Margaret W. Mealy

**152** © 1986, Hope Publishing Co., Carol Stream, IL 60188. All rights reserved. Used by permission.

**153** © 1985, GIA Publications, Inc.

**154** © 1993, GIA Publications, Inc.

**155** Text: © 1983, Japanese United Methodist Church. Tune trans.: © 1983, Abingdon Press (Administered by THE COPYRIGHT COMPANY, Nashville, TN) All Rights Reserved. International Copyright Secured. Used By Permission. Harm.: © 1993, Pilgrim Press

**157** © 1989, GIA Publications, Inc.

**159** Acc.: © 2000, GIA Publications, Inc.

**160** Text: © 1962, World Library Publications, Inc., 3825 N. Willow Rd., Schiller Park, IL 60176. All rights reserved. Used by permission. Harm.: © 1958, Ralph Jusko Publications, Inc.

**161** © 1994, Choristers Guild. Used by permission.

**162** Text and tune: © 1993, Howard S. Olson. Acc.: © 2000, GIA Publications, Inc.

**163** Text and tune adapt.: © 1963, Stainer & Bell, Ltd., London, England. Administered by Hope Publishing Co., Carol Stream, IL 60188. All rights reserved. Used by permission.

**164** © 1986, Bernadette Farrell. Published by OCP Publications. P.O. Box 13248, Portland, OR 97213-0248. All rights reserved. Used with permission.

**165** Text: © 1953, Westminster/John Knox Press. Tune: © 1994, CRC Publications, Grand Rapids, MI 49650. All rights reserved. Used by permission.

**166** Harm.: © 1986, GIA Publications, Inc.

**167** © 1988, GIA Publications, Inc.

# Acknowledgments/*continued*

# Acknowledgments/*continued*

# Index of First Lines and Common Titles/*continued*

# Index of First Lines and Common Titles/*continued*